Mary Chubb was born  joined the staff of the Egypt Exploration Society in London as an under secretary, and two years later was sent out to dig at Tell el Amarna – an experience which inspired a lifelong, if unscholarly, enthusiasm for archaeology. Egypt was followed in 1933 with a season in Iraq, at the site of Tell Asmar, with the Oriental Institute of the University of Chicago, and a short spell in the United States.

Mary Chubb first turned her hand to writing and broadcasting in the 1940s, contributing to *Punch* and working with the BBC. *Nefertiti Lived Here* first appeared in 1954, followed by *City in the Sand*, a colourful account of her experiences of dig life in Iraq.

CITY IN THE SAND

The author. April in Khorsabad.

CITY IN THE SAND

by Mary Chubb

Introduction by Isabel Quigly

This edition published in 1999 by Libri Publications Limited
Suite 281, 37 Store Street
Bloomsbury
London, WC1E 7BS

First published in 1957 by Geoffrey Bles Limited

ISBN 1-901965-02-3

Front Cover: The Mukhtar of Jerwan seated on blocks inscribed with
fragments of the exploits of Sennacherib. Back Cover: Seton and Jake
standing on the aqueduct

Designed and typeset by Libri Publications Limited
Printed and bound in Great Britain by Biddles Limited of Guildford

For
CATHERINE and JON
with my love

Introduction

Who are we? Where do we come from? What formed us? Why are we as we are now? Today's world is amorphous and inexplicable without an idea of the past, including the most ancient, its prehistory. Mary Chubb's *City in the Sand*, reprinted after forty-two years, is about a dig (and several peripheral others) in Iraq in 1932, sandwiched between much shorter accounts of vigorous walking in Greece and Crete with other archaeological friends before and after it. Poignant thoughts arise of then and now in Iraq when she writes, 'The country was at peace, and a good man was king.' Westerners, welcomed and given concessions to dig in certain areas, could plan well ahead and find skilled local labour. As secretary to the Director of the dig, Hans Frankfort, a Dutchman she greatly admired, Mary Chubb was part of an international group funded by the University of Chicago as part of a vast plan of archaeological discovery in the Middle East, stretching forward into the late thirties.

For what became a group not just of colleagues but of friends, it was a time of excitement and intellectual richness, shared and therefore doubled. The main task was the discovery with what seems miraculous skill and luck of Eshnunna, an ancient vassal city of Ur, and its complex uncovering — horizontal layers of building, thirty foot down, sorted into their periods, combed in minutest detail. It was heady work. Seals with which merchants marked their wares told, for instance, how goods had arrived there from India much earlier than anyone had thought; statues identified ancient gods; inscriptions, ancient rulers. Beautiful jewellery, beads, metalware, pottery, tools, artefacts of all sorts testified to the sophisticated civilisation which had ruled there. It was dizzyingly exciting, the daily surprises, the sense of awe, and Miss Chubb, an amateur writing for the general reader, though she learnt a great deal on the way, puts across its fascination to the non-specialist with detailed explanations from the specialists on hand.

Always it is what she calls 'the human touch, a voice speaking down the ages' that appeals most to her: the thought of the man who held the seal 'in his warm brown hand'; of the baby whose perfect footprint was pressed in plaster 'hundreds of years before Abraham, away down in Ur, had gathered up his family and his belongings... to set out westwards for his new homeland'; of the thumb prints on ancient bricks; of the fearsome pear-shaped stones bored through the centre, exactly like those still used by the dig's basket boys as defensive weapons, now mounted on sticks; underground for thousands of years, these wooden handles had perished. As in her earlier book about her first dig, at Tell el-Amarna in Egypt, *Nefertiti Lived Here*, the emphasis in the telling is also on the human story today — that of the team working on the sites: archaeologists, architect, photographer, recorder of objects found, reader of inscriptions, and Gabriel, the indispensable odd-job man and driver who kept the show on the road.

Miss Chubb is a natural stylist, her writing vigorous, fluent and graceful, beautifully paced. Vivid images are slipped in with ease ('the muffled pulsing of the ship's heart'), and descriptions of landscape and weather, particularly in the lovely Greek and Cretan countryside, turn one's heart over now and then. This, of course, is what makes the book most memorable. The subject must fascinate all but the most incurious, and to bring it alive in modern terms there is a group of attractive people in an atmosphere of comradeship, hard work, tough conditions and enormous fun. But it is the writing itself that really brings it alive: Miss Chubb has not just skill with language but a novelist's way with people. The personalities, the day-to-day life, reach us over seventy years as brightly as if they were (as she is) still with us. So her story is not just of great historical interest but an imaginative re-telling of a human one, about young people, their adventures and achievements, the desert and its terrors; above all the past and its gifts to us in the present.

Isabel Quigly, 1999

ILLUSTRATIONS

The illustrations indicated by an asterisk are reproduced by permission of the Director of the Oriental Institute of the University of Chicago.

CHAPTER ONE

THE SECOND NIGHT out from Alexandria the wind dropped, and the little old-fashioned Rumanian ship, which was heading for the Piraeus, gradually rocked to an even keel and went padding gently on her way across the quietening water.

The small cabin was very hot, and I slid out of the narrow bunk, revelling in the welcome steadiness of the deck underfoot. It was about one in the morning, but I had dozed most of the day before through the storm, and by now was very bored with my surroundings. In waking moments I had earnestly studied the pictures of the Rumanian gentleman with a huge moustache getting into his life-jacket in movements A, B and C, and I knew by heart the notices on the back of the door, which had been translated hopefully into English:

> One Siffle is DINNERTIMES!
> Two Siffles is MAN-ON-SEA!!
> Three Siffles is JUMP SHIP!!!

Then there was: 'Passengers please to extinguish all lambs at midnight'—perhaps some folk-Rumanian propitiation of a sea-god? And this *cri-de-cœur* from some clearly all-but-demented musical sea captain: 'Passengers *please* not to play piano in saloon if not play good.'

I put on an overcoat over pyjamas, pushed my feet into Egyptian sandals, and opened the cabin door. Silence in the narrow, white-painted passage-way, except for that familiar ship noise, the quiet, sustained hum, all on one note, of distant machinery, and, just discernible through it, the faint rustle of the wash as it slithered away from the ship and melted back into the unbroken dark water. A single light shone in the deserted lobby amidships, and a sweet salt air flowed in through the open doorways on either side. I stepped into the darkness over the high weather-board on the port side, on to a deck still damp from the spray flung over the rail in the bad weather; and made my way aft.

Magic calm all round—we were gliding through warm emptiness. A very late, honey-coloured moon hung low over the land of Egypt somewhere far astern of us; it was just risen, yet so bright that the sky was luminous and the horizon clear to see all around. Nothing anywhere but the pale, glowing sky and the dark, silken sea—and the muffled pulsing of the ship's heart. Then a light winked suddenly on the port bow, vanished, and shone out again. I stared across the water; and saw that a great shape of grey velvet lay along the sea, a shape with a long, uneven outline drawn against the sky, like a sea-monster watching our passing with a sleepy amber eye. I crossed to the other rail and saw just astern of us another dark mass, black against the path of the moon. A light there, too, close to the water, blinked at us every few seconds. The isles of Greece. This was one of the purely happy moments that I shall always remember: to be quite alone in the softness of a Mediterranean night, with the promise of Greece nearing fulfilment every moment, as already we slipped between her quiet outposts, flashing their messages of safety and welcome. For a long time I leaned on the rail, now watching the islands, now the rising moon, and now the creamy wash streaming along the dark flank of the ship. Was it fancy, or was there already a hint of honey and flowering grass and orange-blossom in the salt air?

It was March in the peaceful thirties; and I was on my way back to London after working in Egypt (for the last time, although I didn't know it) all the winter. I was the secretary to a team sent out by the Egypt Exploration Society each year to excavate the site of Tell el Amarna, the city of Akhenaten. And now I had three weeks' leave due to me, and was going to spend some of it in Greece—to walk again, in good company, through the valleys and over the mountains. Life was very good; and the air was making me overpoweringly sleepy. It would be wonderfully romantic to wait and watch the dawn come up—and surely it would be equally impossible to stay awake a minute longer? I went below and opened my porthole wide; waved to the tip of an island sliding out of sight; crawled into the bunk, and was asleep in a second.

Two days later, three others of the Tell el Amarna staff arrived in Athens from Egypt: John Pendlebury, the Director of the dig, who was at this time also Curator at Knossos, his wife Hilda, and one of the dig architects, Hilary. We laid plans for a walk round part of the Argolid in the Peloponnese, which was new ground for Hilary and me.

"Mycenae, of course," said John, "then south to see Tiryns, with a night or so in Nauplia. Then east to Epidaurus, and on from there perhaps to the east coast at New Epidaurus. We might try getting back to Corinth through the mountains north of Epidaurus—I've never been there. I'll wire to the inn tonight."

He thought we could do the walk in about eight days. We were all sitting in Loubier's on Hermes Street; it was a sort of beerhouse-restaurant, and was a cheerful place to gravitate to as evening fell and the early spring air grew chilly. The beer was pale and cold and memorable, and there was always a plate of savoury snacks thrown in for good measure. Of course, you could have *oozo* if you preferred, but you would prefer only if you liked the taste of aniseed, from which it is made; it is a fiery little drink, wonderful when you are very cold and tired.

Loubier's always seemed to be brimful of laughing Greeks;

and the bustling little waiters in white coats joined in all the jokes. Yet somehow, in the midst of the comfortable warmth and noise and good cheer, I was always conscious that I was in no ordinary city. Quite near where we were sitting, some-where out there beyond the bustle and noise of the lighted streets, the great rock, golden-crested with its splendid frag-ments, towered up into the last of the evening light. Just as when one looks wherever one happens to find oneself in Athens, for a glimpse of the Parthenon, and never fails to find it, whether sailing against the slow clouds or becalmed in a still blue sky, so the modern ways of Athens never seem to obscure or smother beyond recapture the feeling of continuity with her ancient glory. The Acropolis is still her heart; and her life still goes on round and about that heart, even though her people are dwarfed and shadowed by that tremendous symbol of the splendid past.

The next morning we bought things for the trip, which seemed to consist mainly of chocolate and camera-film and in-secticide. In the afternoon John and Hilda went off to the British School to do some work there, and Hilary and I went to the Museum to look at the treasures that Schliemann had found at Mycenae in 1876: the gold diadems and breastplates, the delicate ornaments and carved animals, and above all the golden mask which he had tremblingly raised from the dead face in the shaft grave, the face which he so passionately believed to be that of Agamemnon.

When we left the Museum it was raining: a soft, insistent Grecian benediction; and we slid unashamedly into a Greek movie, until we could decently appear at Loubier's to meet the others. The film was a rendering of the story of Daphnis and Chloe, and the production was just as innocent and disarming. The two beautiful young Greek players acted their parts against incredibly lovely scenery; and nobody, during the filming or later, seemed to have noticed or cared that Daphnis occasionally led his flock along a track accompanied by a telephone wire, or that a distant bus slid at one moment across a corner of the screen. It was a lovely film. We rushed out before the next, probably highly polished, American picture began—the stars of it were named on the screen in Greek lettering as TSON MPARI-MOR and MPILLI DOB. The Greeks get round the problem of the letters which do not exist in their own alphabet as best they can. 'B' they have, but as it is pronounced 'V', it will not do when a foreign word contains 'B' as we sound it. The nearest they can get to it is 'MP'. In the same way, the best they can manage for 'J' is 'TS'. Which is enough to explain which American stars of bygone fame were featured on that rainy day in Athens.

The next afternoon we left on the train bound for the Peloponnese, first through the foothills west of Athens to Eleusis, and then keeping close to the sea along the coast of Megara. Here the land gradually heaves up into rocky heights, and the little train climbed slowly with it, higher and higher, till the fishing-boats were left far below us on the shimmering water. We were dizzily near the edge at moments, and there were times when I gazed out of the landward window and tried not to think of landslides and earthquakes; but the sheer beauty of the view over the sea was too fine to miss. I conquered my qualms and watched the dark tangle of mountain peaks south-ward across the water, which marked the northern shore of the Peloponnese; and looking back the way we had come, could see Salamis lying close to the Attic shore, green and gold in the afternoon sun. We were high enough to see the blue narrows beyond, where a great Persian fleet once sailed to her doom; and beyond that again even the tiny islet of Psittalia, rich in Persian dust; for, as the battle raged on, desperate men, their vessels sunk beneath them, had swum for their lives to it, only to be stoned to death by the pursuing Greeks, flushed with victory, or cut down in their scores as they dragged themselves ashore.

Ahead of us lay the isthmus, and Corinth. Soon we turned south, and crossed the canal by way of the bridge high above the western end of it. Attica and the Saronic Gulf vanished behind a spur of rock, and now we were in the Peloponnese, with the waters of the Gulf of Corinth opening out on our right towards a setting sun. On past Corinth southwards, into the mountainous country. Evening was falling as we puffed and climbed through a twisting pass. Black crags towered up on either side, and little steep valleys fell away from the narrow track. It was very lonely country. Sometimes a still figure holding a crook could be seen standing below us in a steep field near his flock, while his dog raced madly alongside the train, to fend off the snorting dragon come to devour his charges.

The pass widened, and the fearsome crags gave way to gentler hills—the train stopped panting and began to go faster. We were running out of the mountains now; and as we curved downwards through the foothills saw that a great plain stretched away southwards. Far ahead a group of lights twinkled in the dusk.

"Argos," John said.

The train was slowing down now, drawing in to a tiny station several miles short of the once great city of the Argive plain. It stopped; and waited, hissing quietly, while we gathered up ruck-sacks and macs and dropped down to the platform. A single oil lamp swung from the low roof—and it just lit up a tin sign fastened to the wall behind it, giving the name of the station—Mycenae.

The train rumbled off towards Argos, and a young man ran up to John and Hilda, and clasped their hands. This was Spiro, the third of four brothers who kept the Inn of the Fair Helen near the ancient site of Mycenae. They had got John's wire, and Spiro had come to meet us. He led the way out of the station talking excitedly, and we set out along a straight, flat road running due east between black cypresses. The walk had really begun.

We were moving along the foot of the range of mountains which we had just crossed, with high ground to the left, and the plain on our right. Ahead I could make out the dark, high outline of another range running north and south. It had been raining on this side of the mountains, for the road was wet and there was a sound of trickling water at the verge; and the air was full of the scents of pine and damp grass. But the sky was clear, with stars appearing between the marching cypresses. There was no moon; but our shadows leaped and crouched all over the pools in the road, for Spiro was carrying a hurricane lamp. He was a desperately thin young man, with gaunt cheekbones in a sallow face, and a wild tangle of black hair above burning eyes.

After a mile or so a few isolated houses appeared on either side of the road, and then we came to the Inn of the Fair Helen. It stood back from the road on the left, a low white building with its well-known, well-loved name in faded blue letters over the door, where a lamp hung. Spiro stood back for us all to pass in, and then shouted for his brothers. They came in one by one, smiling: Costi, the eldest, a short man with a bad limp, then a young giant called Agamemnon, and then the youngest, Orestes, a blunt-nosed, stocky boy of sixteen. When we had been shown our rooms—reached by a wooden stairway against the back wall of the house—we came down to the long living-room, and settled down for the first of those perfect evenings which happen when you are travelling the hard way through the countryside of Greece. The darkened window, never without its row of deeply interested faces gazing in; the brazier on the floor in the centre of the comfortable circle of hosts and guests and casuals who have dropped in; everyone nursing a little something in a glass—*oozo* or brandy or beer—while the talk rises and falls, and wonderful cooking-scents begin to curl out of the kitchen on the smoky air.

John asked Spiro if he thought he could come with us on the week's walk, and help in various ways, and as guide through the unknown part of the route. Spiro began to say that of course he would, but the two elder men said: "He's been ill—the wet weather will make him bad again—but he'll be all right by summer." Spiro sat silent; then shrugged his thin shoulders, and turned his hands outward in a curiously sad gesture. Then they all agreed that Orestes could go; he was old enough now, they weren't too busy at the inn and it would be a good experience for him, because he wanted to be able to act as guide to travellers walking as we were doing. Why, they said proudly, he knew quite a lot of English already, for this very purpose. Orestes, who was frowning over a small book in a corner, looked up and grinned shyly; and it was fixed that he should come.

Later that evening, when we were alone, we came upon the small book that Orestes had been studying. It was a Greek–English phrase-book, with the English words heroically spelled out in Greek letters, and the phrases themselves almost as inconsequent as the unforgettable: "By heavens! our postilion has been struck by lightning." And of course it was up against the old trouble of 'MP' and 'TS' and so on. 'D', which is pronounced 'Th' in modern Greek, would not do, of course, for English-sounding 'D'; so 'NT' was substituted.

"Ai lä-ik Rampmpits," the author announced suddenly; and then, rather shyly, one felt: "Ntoo you lä-ik Rampmpits?" and continued to harp on the rabbit theme for more than half a page, which made us deeply happy. For the rest of the trip

"Ntoo you lä-ik rabbits?" stood for practically everything, from "Would you like a cigarette?" to "Are you all right?" when a treacherous root had landed you flat on your face in the path, or "Isn't this a heavenly morning?" It was the kind of silly comfortable catch-phrase that seeps into most families; and by now, after the seasons in Egypt, we were on just that kind of footing.

The next morning was dark with cloud, and as we set out eastwards along the road, a fine drizzle began; but we went free of travelling gear, because we were coming back for one more night to the inn. Soon we bore to the left and began climbing, as the road curved round a great hill. Now we had our backs to the plain, and were climbing into a large amphitheatre shut in closely on three sides by craggy rocks. How high they soared could not be seen, for the mist was drifting low about them. The track, always rising, now turned to the right, following the U-shaped contour of the mountains right round until it seemed to come to a full stop against the mountain-side across the steep valley. Down in that misty hollow where the ground fell away from the track lay huge, dark, glistening blocks of masonry in the grass. There seemed to be only the four of us in the world that morning, as we went up the track, bearing right all the way until at last we reached the end of it where it ran between huge ruined walls. Across the path now a mighty barrier loomed through the mist—solid mountain rock, it seemed; but as we drew nearer, the central part of it grew paler, and thinned away into emptiness. We had come up to the Lion Gate of Mycenae.

Above the stupendous lintel, cut from a single block, towered the twin heraldic lions on either side of the tapering central pillar, as they had stood for more than 2000 years. For a few moments no one spoke; and we stood in that strange place, the threshold of Agamemnon's stronghold, while the mist drifted through the gateway and streamed past us down the track, like the wraiths of the ancient warriors setting out again towards the sea, towards distant Troy, towards vengeance.

"I think this is rather the right kind of day to see this place for the first time," Hilary said slowly. John moved forward towards the small modern rail-gate which barred the way in—the guard in the village had handed him over the key, as he was a privileged archaeologist. He made a proud face. "I feel very majestic holding the key of Mycenae in my hand." He spoke banteringly; but I was sure that, as he often did, he had thrown his inflection like a light cloak round a thought which was anything but frivolous.

We moved under the shadowy gateway, into the citadel-fortress. There to the right, all among the wet grass and flowers, was the double circle of vertical stone slabs, wherein Schliemann had found the shaft-graves; and where, peering down into their dim cavities, he pierced again the fairy veil of legend, and found that, as he had always believed, historical truth lay at its heart.

We climbed to the great summit of the Citadel, over the fragments of colossal walls, up to the shadowy halls of Agamemnon. Up there, high above the Gateway, where pillar bases and doorways, built 1000 years and more before the days of classical Greece, can still clearly be seen, perhaps that faithless wife, Clytemnestra, and her lover Aegistheus had watched for the signal beacons which would warn them that the hero had returned from Troy and was even now approaching from the coast. Here perhaps, close to this sunken hearth where we were standing, he may have fallen, struck down even as she spoke the first false words of greeting.

· · · · · ·

The next day we set out for Tiryns, due south, in bright sunshine, with Orestes. The mountain peaks around Mycenae were very high and clear now, red brown against the still blue. We passed through small villages of white houses, set among groves of oranges and lemons, gold and topaz gleaming through the dark leaves. I hadn't got a walking-stick, and presently Orestes brought me one which he had cut from a roadside thicket; he had whittled it smooth as he walked, and had shaped a curly crook handle with a hole through it to fit on to the head of the stick. "Yia Thespeena Maria—for Mees Mary," he said courteously, as he handed it over; and I realised with delight that Thespeena was just the same word, pronounced differently, as the 'Despoina'—'Lady'—of classical times and drama. That crook hangs on the wall of my room to this day.

So we came to Tiryns, a huge limestone crag rising up out of the flat plain, crowned with its fortress-walls of colossal thickness. Legend spoke of it as the birthplace of Herakles; legend affirmed that Proetus was King of Tiryns, that seven giant Cyclops had put the huge polygonal blocks together to make the walls. But until 1884 archaeologists dismissed the ruins as medieval and not worth investigation—all of them, that is, except Schliemann, still following single-heartedly his instinct that somewhere behind the fantasies of legend he would find history. In that year he came to Tiryns, and digging on its high crest found the remains of a palace more splendid than any yet found, surrounded by tremendous fortification walls. And as for being medieval—his finds, and particularly the pottery, proved beyond a doubt that Tiryns was as old as Mycenae, a mighty palace-fortress built by some great Greek prince as early as 1500 B.C. It is the earliest European castle with outer walls of stone.

We climbed up the steep ramp cut in the rock; it was cunningly sited so that an enemy came up with his vulnerable side (the right) towards the defenders, his shield being on his left arm. Through the main gate, and then between double walls so close-set there was scarcely room to pass. The inner sides of these walls glistened in the shadow, and John said that it was due to the countless generations of sheep straying up and down the mound, and polishing the walls with the oil in their woolly coats as they slowly rubbed along, nibbling at the flowers and grass.

Now we emerged on to the airy plateau, and wandered through the outer bailey, where the stables and storerooms had been placed, then through the remains of a great gateway to the palace courtyard which faced the once-pillared entrance to the main hall. Rooms led off this hall, including a bathroom with a sunken bath and drain.

All around stretched the green plain, surrounded on three sides by the mountains; to the north the clouds had gathered again over Mycenae, and the mountains there hung dark and threatening. To the south, quite near, lay the sea, brilliantly blue; and across the bay on which Nauplia stands rose the mountains of Sparta, their snows reflected in the quiet water. A light wind stirred, and the little wind-flowers all over the ruins danced and nodded to the faint tune. Far down on the white road a shepherd was moving northwards, a small flock at his heels, along the road that Agamemnon himself may have taken to his doom.

We went down another way that John knew about, on the western flank of the crag, a secret way that had been made so that men could slip in and out unseen in troubled times; it was a passage cut through the rock and ending in a steep flight of steps. As evening fell, we marched into Nauplia; and found rooms in a little house on the edge of the water looking out to the Venetian castle in the bay.

The hard beds didn't do much to ease tired limbs, and it was good to set out next morning very early, after a breakfast of coffee and bread and goat's-milk butter, towards Epidaurus, which lies near the east coast of the Argolid. But stiffness and a bad night were forgotten in five minutes of swift walking and heavenly scenery and gay company. There wasn't a real road. Sometimes we were in a valley, following a brown stream which wound through silver olive-groves. The vivid grass was splashed with the scarlet, mauve and white of anemones, with graceful swaying heads of dusty pink asphodel. Patches of red ploughland glowed among the green pasture. Everywhere there was the scent of flowers and herbs, the sound of water, mingling with tinkling goat-bells, or the patter of donkeys' hooves as the little creatures, loaded with brushwood, picked their way neatly past us along the track. Sometimes we were struggling up a bleak hillside as the country grew wilder.

In the midst of all this beauty lies Epidaurus, where we came in the late afternoon. We were moving beneath a grove of pines when the sun, striking through it, lit up a marble block lying in the grass; then another, and another, until soon we were picking our way slowly through widespread ruins. And as John and Hilda began to point out and explain the complex buildings all about us, the dread shadow of Tiryns and Mycenae, the sense of doom and danger and death which they had evoked, and which had yet lingered with me all this lovely day, lifted; for as we walked about the delicate gleaming ruins of Epidaurus, we slipped backward in time a thousand years, to an age of high culture, to a civilised time of learning and leisure and laughter. Here in classical times a kind of health-centre had come into being, a shrine of Aesculapius, with baths and temples and rest-houses. As it grew in extent, inevitably the Greeks built a stadium for sporting contests; and there we could see its dead-level floor, out beyond the trees, still with its tiers of gleaming white seats along each side for the spectators. But with the Greeks this delight in physical perfection and prowess was never enough to satisfy their leisure hours; the joys of the mind ranked higher; and here, not far from the stadium, are the remains of the largest and finest theatre in all Greece. It lies in a great hollow of the hill which curves about the town, with sixty tiers of seats, which could accommodate many thousands of playgoers. The topmost tier is very far from and high above the circular space where the actors played their parts; but the semicircular, fan-like shape of the auditorium produced such perfect acoustics that the actors had no need to raise their voices to be heard at the furthest point of it. We tried it, and found that even a match struck far away down on the stage sounded as if it were close to the ear.

Late that evening we breasted a low wooded hill and came down a gentle slope to New Epidaurus, on the eastern shore of the Peloponnese. Lights twinkled on the calm water where fishing caïques still lay, and in the cluster of small houses grouped round the quayside. A few men on the quay were talking and smoking near their boats, but they fell silent and stared as the five strangers came slowly and—in one case at least—limpingly down the track between the trees. But of course they were used to the strange folk of other lands, who were prepared to walk for countless kilos, or come on mule-back, or even dare the perils of bouncing over the unmade roads in motor-cars in order to see the ancient stones of their country. And every year many of the walkers found their way further on to their little community after exploring the ancient nearby ruins, seeking food and shelter, instead of going back to Nauplia.

In a minute they had taken the business of where to eat and sleep out of our hands, and were having a lovely competition as to which of them should put us up, with John and Hilda and Orestes chipping in whenever they got a chance, while Hilary and I subsided on to the low sea-wall, Hilary murmuring occasionally: "It's my knee-caps." In my case it was an outsize

14

blister on one heel, which had begun needling into my conscious-ness just before we got to the site, and had been occupying my entire attention very forcibly during the last mile or so. But I knew what he meant. So much of walking in Greece is done vertically, whether it is a short clamber or a long mountain, that the knees seem to take much more of the strain than ankles and feet. Downhill was worse than up.

But to sit and relax, and know that you had reached your goal for the day, to watch the still water, and the huge quiet mountains protecting the bay, with the sound of Greek laughter and banter in your ears, and the memory of all the beauty you had passed through during the day—this was the kind of mo-ment so good that somehow the aches and a raw heel seemed to be part of the joy of it, and make it even better.

After a time the meeting broke up and we were led to a house on the water's edge by a lean old salt, and were greeted by his brown and beaming wife, swathed in a black shawl, while Orestes went off somewhere with his new buddies. For a while we sat blissfully silent, eating little black olives, in a tiny parlour almost filled by a table covered with a red plush cloth and supporting a huge oil lamp of archaic design. But soon we were eating wonderful fresh-caught fish, fried up with little bits of octopus-tentacle, and drinking the pale resinated wine of Greece with the strange flavour which always made me think of the sharp scent of chrysanthemums.

We rested for two days in that lovely place, while muscles unwound themselves and blisters healed, swimming round the gaily painted caïques in the tiny harbour, and dozing under the sunlit olives on the green slopes. Then we set out early one morning northward, to find a way through to the north coast of the Peloponnese; and at once began climbing into grandly mountainous and lonely country. John and Hilda had never been here before, and young Orestes had never been east of

Nauplia. The good folk of New Epidaurus knew of a village called Sophiko somewhere to the north of them in the high mountains; but only mule-tracks led that way, and they were quite hazy as to how many hours' walking it would take to get there. No one in Greece dreams of giving the distance to a place in mileage, for the very sensible reason that vertical and horizontal miles take different times to walk. Time is the only measuring-rod that is of any practical use. John found Sophiko on his map, and it appeared to be only about ten miles away—but, as he said cheerfully, that didn't mean a thing, as the contours showed that it looked like being very difficult country ahead.

And so it was. All day we followed a mule-track, twisting and climbing and dropping, and lost count of the little hidden valleys and the bleak upland shoulders which we put behind us. Late in the afternoon we were high on the flank of a mountain on the western side of a deep, steep valley dropping away on our right for a thousand feet or so. John sat down with his feet over the edge and brought out his map. We had not seen another human being or passed a house all day. "We *ought* to be about here," he said dubiously, pointing, "but I really am not sure which of these valleys we have got into." Orestes naturally hadn't a clue—he looked startled that his own country could seem so ominously unfamiliar. We went on in single file, watching the shadow of our own mountain creep higher up the flank of the one across the valley; the sun was well on the way to bed. It would be quite difficult to keep to the rough track once it was dark, and far from pleasant if it came to spending a chilly March night out in the open.

Then, as we rounded a corner, we heard a sudden sound coming across the valley—a woodman's axe. It stopped; the owner of the axe had probably spotted us and was watching the unusual sight of five people on foot, without a mule, moving along his valley. Orestes hailed him. "How far to Sophiko?" A voice rang out through the trees. "Eh—about two hours; but you're on the wrong side of the valley—you'll have to go back." The foot of the valley was miles behind us. "Is there a track your side?" "*Malista, malista*, yes, yes, indeed—along the trees, there." We could see it then—a faint scar in the green, almost as high as we were. "We *can't* go back, John," Hilda said. "It'll be dark soon—let's risk it and slither." We peered down the steep side of the mountain to its dark, tangled depths —but anything was better than going back. We dropped off the track and began to slide down the steep slope through rocks and saplings, at times a good deal faster than was healthy. Luckily there were no unseen sheer drops or rushing waters at the bottom of it. We reached ground level unhurt, if breathless and scratched, and with very fine highlights on the seats of skirts and trousers. Then began the struggle up the other side. All this time the axe was silent; but as we hauled ourselves up on to the new track in safety, we heard the chopping begin again merrily, so that we must have had a hidden and deeply interested eye on us all the time. It was an odd and happy feeling to have been guided and watched by someone you never set eyes on.

There was more light on this side of the valley, and we stepped out with renewed confidence, but with tiring bodies. Orestes looked as if he were wondering if the occupation of guide was all that he had thought. As it grew darker our spirits began to wilt. Orestes strode ahead as if it were a matter of personal honour to produce a missing village for us. Clouds began drifting overhead, and a chilly wind moaned past us. When we had walked a good deal longer than the woodman's two hours, and were rounding one more jutting outcrop, John suggested creeping up very quietly and seeing if we could perhaps catch it unawares. We turned the corner and gazed into the depths of another empty valley, this time running across our path, with a great mountain soaring up beyond it—not a light anywhere, not a hint of wood smoke or warmth or humankind. Our own path now swung away to the right. Then we saw Orestes far away in that direction against the skyline—he had climbed a high rock alongside the path to get a better view. He was waving his hat and pointing away further on where we couldn't see. We slogged after him. The sole was coming off my right shoe. It was almost dark, and we stumbled along over the boulders towards the stocky silhouette. John and Hilda were ahead, and as Hilary and I came up to the three of them as they stood, John was murmuring: "Oh, lovely—lovely!" Across the valley from us, high on a mountain ledge, but not really very far distant, lay a cluster of little white-and-brown houses, pricked with lights. Orestes had found Sophiko for us.

Downhill once more; and as we crossed the narrow valley, we fell in with some villagers, homeward bound: women with donkeys loaded with brushwood, shepherds and goatherds, all making for food and shelter and rest. The wide, zigzag path up to the village was easy after the stony track we had trod, and by the time we had reached the cobbled street, John had learned from our companions where to find an inn to shelter us for the night. It was quite dark now; as we came to the lighted door of the *Taverna*, escorted by most of the population, I looked back for a moment over the low parapet wall at the side of the street, a very useful parapet in a place like that, for without it the villagers would have been constantly falling off into the view. The great mountains southward towered against the stars; and as I turned into the gloriously warm stuffiness of the inn, and the old wooden door creaked shut after us, I knew the primitive joy of gaining, as a treasured prize, the most basic thing in life: warmth and shelter. And soon swollen knees and ankles were throbbing comfortably, close to a blazing brazier, and fiery spirits were whispering cheerful messages down chilly throats, and the good people of the inn were shouting their heads off over the details of our coming supper; and a splendid old gentleman in a cloak and high boots was asking innumerable questions about our journey and our business and our destination and our families—and of course the window was blocked solid with dark, intent faces.

The next morning John discovered that at the other end of the village, unlikely as it seemed, there was a real road—almost —which led away northward through the mountains to Corinth; and along this road a bus travelled twice a week. We decided that yesterday's walk was worthy of three normal ones, and felt that a bus-ride had been honourably earned. Also Hilary and I were supposed to be catching a boat that left Piraeus in three days' time; also no amount of string and ingenious repairs and knots by Hilary would keep the two halves of my right shoe together now for more than half an hour. So, as our host had said that there would be a bus leaving that day at about eleven in the morning, we went and sat in a row in the sun in the little cobbled square and waited. Nothing happened for an hour, and then an ancient Sophikoan wandered up and explained that the bus didn't *start* from here; it started from Corinth, and anything might have happened to it on the way up. We went back to the inn and asked for some food; and while we were in the middle of eating it there was a noise outside like cavalry doing a musical ride over sheets of corrugated iron. We ran out, and there was a small, ramshackle bus in the very middle of the square, with steam pouring out of all its joints, and about fifty people, it seemed, pouring out of its door. We ran back to the inn and madly paid the bill for the lunch, and ran out to the bus, with me at the back of the party going ker-flip, ker-flap—another piece of string had come adrift. I passed Hilary tearing back to the inn. "First we run one way, and then we run the other," he shouted with his mouth full. "Nearly left my perishing camera behind." It was now about 1.30. The driver had vanished, and the same ancient as before told us that it was very, very difficult driving up from Corinth, and the driver had to have some food and a nice sleep before he went back there. We went and sat in a row in the sun in the little cobbled square, and waited. . . . After an hour or so a rumour seeped round somehow that the driver was still asleep and most likely wouldn't feel like going back to Corinth that day at all. But in the morning: "Very, very early—*proï, proï.*" We went back to the inn.

'Very, very early next morning' turned out to be 11.30, when we joined the throng who were trying to get into the bus. We set off much too loaded up for safety, I thought, as we bumped over the cobbles and then swung off on to the road round a spur of hill; and little Sophiko vanished from sight for ever. I noticed nervously that several ladies among the passengers crossed themselves as they embarked. "And with good reason," said John; "but the drivers are usually inspired in this country. You needn't feel really nervous until you see me beginning to tremble." It didn't make me feel very happy. I think we coasted most of the way, going much too fast round hairpin bends with dizzy depths below them, and bouncing over the remains of landslides which occasionally bestrewed the path. One of the front springs went at one point, and we crunched and lurched to a crawl, while all the men jumped out and ran along in front trying to see what was the matter. They looked like the Lost Boys scaring wolves the way Peter had shown them, by look-ing at them upside down between their knees. The excitement was intense. At last they managed to break the bit off which was dangling down and scraping along the road, and climbed back into their places, carrying the relic, all arguing happily. The driver let in the clutch, taking both hands off the wheel to turn them outwards in beautiful Grecian resignation. "So long as it isn't a vital piece of brake," Hilda said with her eyes shut as we gathered speed and flicked round the next bend.

Then suddenly there was the sea again; we were looking down from a great height on the waters on either side of the Isthmus of Corinth. Far away to the north-east we could see the line of Hymettus hanging above Athens; and there to the north-west, beyond the turquoise, white-capped waves of the Gulf of Corinth, rose the glittering peaks of Parnassos, snow covered, against a sky of heavenly blue.

We had come full circle round this corner of the Argolid. A few hours later we were waving good-bye to Orestes as he stood on the edge of the small platform at Corinth; for we had just caught the only train of the day, as it was on the point of puffing off on its long pull round the coast back to Athens. There he stood, becoming smaller and darker and somehow more lonely looking every minute, as we headed off towards the Canal; but he was beaming as he went on waving his hat; was he not now a guide? He had found Sophiko; and now he was on his way back to find his brothers and his daily work in the inn, and his little phrase-book—all waiting there for him under the mighty shadow of golden Mycenae.

.   .   .   .   .   .

"Crete next year," John called out from the quay at Piraeus, two days later, as the ship drew away and swung slowly round towards the harbour mouth. Crete next year. It wasn't all over —I would come back to this magical place of warm sun and snow-peaks, of sea and red earth and honey-scented air, swing along its valleys and struggle over its uplands again. It was a consoling thought as Hilary and I travelled northwards; a warming thought as we landed at Venice, which was deep in snow, an unfamiliar Venice drawn all in black and white; we shivered, hunched in overcoats, as a small launch took us from the ship to the station, chugging along the still, black waterways between silent walls and closed doorways and shuttered grilles, and beneath empty bridges, all fantastically etched and pointed under their new-fallen trappings of silvery white. The dry splendour of the sun in Egypt, the sparkle of the Greek springtime seemed very far away now. On we went northward.

London was raw and bleak. But it wasn't only the weather that chilled my spirits those first days, contending with gritty winds and sooty showers and the pale-faced, hurrying crowds, while the first of the barrows of spring flowers went trundling bravely along Oxford Street. There they were, the saffron clouds of mimosa, the tight little wistful bunches of anemones and the gay platoons of tulips. I couldn't look at the anemones without a pang, without a sudden memory of a green pasture beneath an olive-grove, over which some Greek god had flung out a myriad jewels and left them blazing in the grass. No, it wasn't only the weather—for one thing, there was a small paragraph in *The Times* one day reporting a severe earthquake tremor in Greece, during which a small village in the north-east of the Peloponnese, named Sophiko, had been entirely destroyed. For another, the news at the office when I reported back for work seemed to lower the temperature still further; the air was full of the need for retrenchment and dire economies, for a few years at least. The dig at Tell el Amarna would be closed down almost certainly; and in that case it was unlikely that two secretaries would be employed in the London office.

How foolish I'd been to imagine that such an enchanting pattern would go on indefinitely. London—Egypt—Greece; London—Egypt—Crete; London—Egypt—where next? No, it was finished; and I had better begin looking for a normal secretarial job, where I should be lucky if the pattern didn't boil down to something pretty conventional sandwiched between two journeys daily by Underground, in the rush-hour. Well, why not? Why should I expect so much more than the usual secretarial job? I suppose I had been spoiled by too much golden luck, dazzled by too much golden sunshine. Crete next year? No—it was all over.

CHAPTER TWO

THE LAST WEEKS in the London office slipped away. The dusty leaves of the plane-trees in Tavistock Square drooped in the summer heat, moving only as the buses rumbled by and stirred the air; already they were beginning to darken towards their autumn brown. I was still half-heartedly reading advertisements called 'Secretaries Wanted'; tactful, cheerful, book-keeping-not-essential secretaries, secretaries who could drive a car, or comb a dog, or read proofs in Erse, or take a maniac relative out for walks. There didn't seem to be any demand for secretaries who liked listening to Egyptian workmen singing as they dug up ancient temples; for secretaries who liked sitting by braziers in Greek taverns. Half-heartedly I followed up a few of the advertisements, and was always thankful when, for some reason or another, I found myself out on the pavement after an interview, still breathing freely. Although I knew very well that it was almost impossible that I would find another job in field-archaeology of the same kind—for English excavations were always beset with the problem of how to stretch inadequate funds further than they could possibly go—I was haunted by the thought of getting involved in a normal post, however pleasant it might turn out to be, cutting myself off from the happiness I had known, and then, when it was just too late, hearing that the miracle had happened, that someone like me was needed on a dig, and that I had lost my chance.

At last I knew that I must give up this hopeless hang-fire policy, and get on with it. I took an hour off before lunch one day and went down to the City to see the manager of the distributing warehouse of a famous firm which made suede goods, mostly gloves and jackets. He appeared to crave secretarial help somewhere down Wood Street, which leads off Cheapside. It might be fun to work in the City, I told myself—adding, to make it sound more romantic, under the very shadow of St. Paul's.

Mr. Ommaney was a surprise. I had expected the manager of a big concern like this to be scarlet and square and severe; he was very thin and pale and gentle. He interviewed me in a tiny office off the main floor of the warehouse, which was like a huge shop without any customers. Two wide counters ran the length of it on either side of the entrance door, and the shelved walls behind them were packed solid with white cardboard boxes. The space between the counters and the shelves was filled with men pushing step-ladders about, running up and down the ladders, dragging boxes off the shelves, uttering strange yells and dropping the boxes with a crash on to the counters. Other men were yanking the boxes off the counters with further yells, and running away with them into the far distance. I noticed the labels on one or two of the boxes as I passed. One of them said: "Handsewn Nutria Prickseam Velbex Gauntlets". It looked as if I should have to invent some new shorthand. The noise was muffled a little in the office, but I noticed that Mr. Ommaney shut his eyes at every crash, and lost his end of the conversation. He had a very quiet voice, and only spoke between crashes. He told me that he had just recovered from a nervous breakdown. He badly wanted help with the written work, which was heavy, and beyond the capacity of the young typists in the invoice department. "I'm sure you won't notice the noise after a few days." I felt a wave of panic at his assumption that I was going to take the job. "I should want you to go to Worcester quite often, where the factory is," he said in a lull. "That would make a nice change for you sometimes from—here." (Wallop!

"Come on, *come on*, COME ON, boy! Clear that perishing lot—look lively—Come ON!" Thud, thud, wallop!)

"They *are* long hours, I know, but I think you'll agree the money is quite good," he murmured apologetically. It was. "And I do very badly need someone to take off all the written work I have to get through—someone who can write proper English." I wondered, gazing at his anxious, wrinkled brow, how you wrote proper English about Handsewn Nutria Prickseam Velbex Gauntlets. I said that I would think it over. My eye wandered to an enchanting suede waistcoat of soft yellow (ladies) displayed on a stand that I could see through the glass door. "The Staff can have any of our goods at cost price," came a faint whisper across the desk. "D'you think you could start on August 1st?" I said again I would think it over. We moved again through the double hailstorm of white boxes to the street door. We shook hands, and he faded back into his strange kingdom.

As I circled St. Paul's in a bus that was heading back to Holborn, I thought that I would take the job; anyway for a while. It was a queer one, but I liked Mr. Ommaney; there was something in it beyond just a job—I might be able to make the difference for him between recovering his nerve, getting his work and his life under control again, or heading off on another crack-up, which would probably be the end this time of his responsible job. Probably he had an anxious wife somewhere, worrying about him. After all, it was also a good job for me—buttoned into an endless procession of gaily-coloured waistcoats for the rest of time, if I liked. I got off the bus at Kingsway and turned northwards. But by the time I had got as far as Southampton Row, I knew that I was deceiving myself. Inwardly I was hating the idea of the whole thing, the daily struggle in congested buses or tubes to Wood Street and back, in all weathers; the city crowds, the darkness and noise of the warehouse, the routine work. At Russell Square I was thinking about those waistcoats, and of Mr. Ommaney's thinly-thatched top-knot above his kind brown eyes. As I reached the office door on the first floor of the house in Tavistock Square, I decided to ring him up after the lunch hour and say that I would start in August.

The Secretary of the Society wasn't back from her lunch yet; but the office door was unlocked, which probably meant that some member had come in to read in the Library before she left. I was glad that there was someone there to distract my thoughts until it would be time to ring up. It might simply be one of the young Associate-Members, a boy student, snatching a few happy moments in his lunch-hour to look up some Egyptological facts; or an ancient—perhaps celebrated—scholar, teetering along the bookshelves in search of some wanted tome. There was the sound of a book shutting, and I walked through to see who was there.

I saw neither the callow boy nor the greybeard. I saw a slight, dark-haired, clean-shaven man in a brown suit; dark eyes beneath a powerful brow. He was standing with a large book in his hands, watching the door to see who was coming, alert, his head a little cocked.

"Oh! hullo, Hans," I said.

"It is you—goot!" he said. "I wanted to see you." He swung round quickly to the bookshelves, slid the book into place and turned back to me.

Hans Frankfort was already, at the age of thirty-five, very well known in the world of archaeology. He was a Dutchman, who as a student had come from Holland to work under Sir Flinders Petrie. It was a small book of Petrie's about the aims and scope of archaeology, read by chance, that had first kindled his ambition to become an archaeologist himself. To gain his first experience of field-work, Petrie found him a place as Field

Assistant on a prehistoric site in Egypt. Swiftly he began to amass the knowledge and material for his first publication, a comparative study of the pottery of the Ancient Near East. It is a standard work to this day. He had been the Field Director at Tell el Amarna the year before John Pendlebury. Now he was the Field Director of the Iraq Expedition of the Oriental Institute of the University of Chicago. The founder and director of the Oriental Institute, James Henry Breasted, travelling through Egypt in company with John D. Rockefeller Jr. a few years earlier, had visited him at Tell el Amarna. Not long after his return to Chicago he wrote to him to ask if he would take over the leadership of the expeditions in Mesopotamia that formed part of the huge archaeological campaign being carried out by the Oriental Institute, with Rockefeller's support.

"I heard that you are leaving here," he said.

"Yes," I answered sadly. "I *think* it's only due to finance; they seemed to think I was useful out there."

Hans produced a wonderful Dutch expletive full of soft gutturals, which often happened when he was excited.

"Of course you were useful—all digs should have secretaries —why such diffidence?"

I mentioned that I was feeling extremely diffident at the moment.

"Ah!" he said quietly. Then: "I hear from Chicago that they cannot, and will not, stand my typing or book-keeping for one more season."

I thought of Hans' typing, which I had frequently had to unscramble when he had sent reports back from Egypt—and decided that Chicago had got something.

"Last season," he went on, "Jake and I tried to do all the accounts—four months of them—in one day in the train between Antioch and Stamboul. Chicago did not like the result."

"Who is Jake?" I asked politely, looking carefully away from a sudden wild surmise that was making my heart jump about in an odd way. Hans was not given to reminiscing pointlessly.

"He is a brilliant Sumerian scholar—but not a very good accountant. Neither am I—we had the hell of a time, and ended up with about a thousand dollars in a column which we had to invent called 'Inexplicable Items'."

I laughed for the first time in weeks, but a bit shakily.

"Well, what are you going to do about it, Hans? It's a shocking waste of a scholar's time to have to do that side of the work. I really think I proved that at Amarna. It ought to be done properly, and it takes a lot of time."

"Exactly," he said. "And so I have told them. I wrote to Chicago about it weeks ago—and they fervently agree." (It can't, it can't, it *can't* be going to happen.) "I want to know if you will come out as my secretary, and do just what you did at Amarna. We go back in October—think it over for a day or two."

"I don't need to think it over for a day or two," I said. "I'm coming."

. . . . . .

My first step in the direction of Mesopotamia was half a mile southward from Tavistock Square. The London office of the Iraq Expedition was a small room on the top floor of an inconspicuous block of offices in the little oblique cut-through connecting Kingsway and Hart Street, known as Sicilian Avenue. Here in London, since Hans lived in Hampstead and not in Chicago, all the work was done after each season in the field, the work of preparing the season's results for publication in Chicago. Although the office was small it was very bright and ship-shape. The outer wall was all window, which let in maximum light on to the drawing-table running below it. When I made my first appearance there at the beginning of

September, a tall, thin young man was leaning over a sloping drawing-board under the window. This was Seton Lloyd, whom I already knew. He was an architect by training, now applying his knowledge of building, and skill in drawing, to the task of unravelling the tangled ruins of an ancient civilisation, and in the process rapidly becoming an archaeologist in his own right. He, too, had worked at Tell el Amarna, which somehow helped to make me feel less homesick. Now he turned to say 'Hullo', looking down at me from his thin, elegant height, his normally withdrawn expression warmed for the moment by a friendly smile. "I wonder how you will like it," he said, "after Amarna." It was good to think that he had the image of that lovely place behind his eyes, the wide, shining river, the palm-groves, the golden cliffs.

"How does it compare with Amarna?" I asked. "I don't know a thing about it."

He turned back to his drawing, and stood looking down at it, consideringly, eyes half-shut above high cheekbones, T-square in one hand, cigarette in the other.

"You can't compare them," he said. "I hope you won't hate it—no trees, no water, no cultivation; it is incredibly remote."

It didn't sound inviting—and the few photographs on the walls didn't do anything to contradict this bleak summary. One, clearly taken from the air, looked like an astronomer's map of Mars with its canals; an expanse of rough, pockmarked ground criss-crossed here and there with sharp, dark lines.

"That's the ruler's Palace," said Seton, pointing to the lower group of clear-cut lines. "And here,"—his long finger moving up to another group—"are the private houses of the city: you can see the main street *there*; if you look closely you can see the lines of more walls running under the sand, which haven't been dug yet; you can only see them from the air, not on the ground at all. And *that*," he added, indicating a square building at the bottom edge of the photograph, which actually seemed to have a roof on it, "is the Expedition House. The Air Force boys out there did this air-view for us; isn't it a lovely job?" It was certainly interesting, if not, to my mind, exactly lovely, and I said so; but I didn't add, "What city are we talking about, anyway?" I felt sure he would have had such a shock. I decided to do some reading before I began to ask silly questions.

"This drawing I'm doing now is a section through the Palace I showed you; at least as far down as we have got." I peered at it respectfully. The drawing was divided into several horizontal strips, each one with a Roman numeral in it, like a Plimsoll line.

"What exactly——?"

"The layers? Each one represents a different building period; each ruler kept on rebuilding, according to his ideas and needs, on the earlier foundations. Very different from Amarna, isn't it, with its single building period? It is incredibly complicated digging."

Incredibly remote, incredibly complicated. I felt chilled at this introduction to the unknown venture ahead. Then Hans came in, and the bleak feeling of being an ignorant outsider receded a little.

"I have an odd piece of work for you before we leave next month," he said cheerfully. "I want you to take your little shorthand pad and depart to the wilds of Hampstead each morning, beginning tomorrow. There you will find Pierre—he has something in his head which must somehow be got out of it and down on paper before the new season begins. But he knows very little English—you can help him. Find out what he wants to put, and then put it—yes?"

"Yes," I said doubtfully.

"Goot!" said Hans.

For the next month I sat each morning in a small, bow-fronted house in Fitzjohn's Avenue opposite a small, bow-fronted Russian, while he dug out of himself a monograph about something called the Planoconvex Brick. By the time I landed up in Mesopotamia I knew quite a lot about the Plano-convex Brick—quite apart from how to spell it in shorthand—and nothing at all about anything else to do with the dig. For the first week or so it was very hard work. Pierre knew exactly what he wanted to say, but couldn't say it; and I could prob-ably have said it if I had had any idea of what he was talking about. He was very shy about the language difficulty. Hans had told me that he had a genius for practical field work, and had a lot to say about the significance of the aforesaid brick, which was made and used only at one period during the history of Sumer. It was made by filling a small rectangular wooden frame, which was placed on a flat piece of ground, as full as it would go with soft clay mixed with chopped straw, pressed well down and then roughly smoothed off on top with the hand; the frame was then lifted off, and the brick left to bake hard in the sun. Pierre, of course, had lots of photographs of them, which he showed me; and something tingled in me when I made out the impressions on the top of them of thumbs and fingers, left there by the ancient brickmakers as they had pushed the soft brick out of the frame. As the top of the brick was usually left rather rounded—like a slightly risen tin loaf—archaeologists had invented this term for this particular kind of brick; plano- of course referring to the flat underside, and convex to the rounded top. The queer shape made them awk-ward for the ancient builders to use flat in the normal way; and among other things Pierre wanted to record the various methods of wall construction where these bricks were found.

"First, deez breeks vos laid on etch, leaningk to zee left, next deez odder breeks above, like deez below, on etch, but deez lean zee odder way, to zee r-r-right."

My shorthand became very wild as I chased after the bricks, first one way, then the other.

"Zey are leaning different ways on zee etches from demselves—'ow you say?"

" 'Erringkbone," I said earnestly. It was very catching.

" *'Erringkbone?* Vot is, pliz?"

"Zey lean on zee etches—I mean—look, like this . . ." and sketched on my pad a herring having an X-ray photograph.

"Ah! *so*—yes—'erringkbone." Pierre beamed at me, brown eyes gleaming behind flashing glasses. We pressed on.

.   .   .   .   .   .

A few weeks later I was driving down from Jerusalem to the airfield at Ramleh, near the coast, to meet Hans and his wife Yettie, their three-year-old son Jon, and Pierre, who had all just arrived by sea; and then we were going to fly to Baghdad together, some 600 miles to the east. I was with Rachel Levy; we had travelled out from England together, and had spent a week in Jerusalem. Rachel took care of all the objects that were found on the site; but, as I knew already from experience, the work of any one member of the staff usually went far beyond the scope of the technical job which he or she had been engaged to do primarily. In Rachel's case it went far deeper as well; for she had a great knowledge of the Ancient Near East; knowledge that enriched all the discussions which evolved among the specialists from the events of the dig, when a new find, perhaps, or new evidence in some building appeared to confirm or confound some theory in the making.

I had never flown before, and thought that the huge silver plane looked reassuringly solid as our car turned off the airfield tarmac and bumped over the grass towards it. But the car didn't seem to be stopping; it circled the monster's tail, and drew up on the far side, where a small group of officials were standing talking to our own party, close to a tiny cabin monoplane looking like a pilot-fish sheltering in the shadow of a shark. My heart sank. It seemed that the other plane had just flown in from the Far East; if only it hadn't been there, ours might have looked a little less flimsy. We climbed in; there were only eight passenger seats, so that it was mostly a dig party. Jon sat on Yettie's knee opposite, and gazed solemnly at me. He had a beret on the back of his head, and was holding a bright green rubber crocodile which was blown up to bursting point. Pierre settled himself, beaming, in front of me, much happier than I had yet seen him—it must be all those planoconvex bricks he would soon be seeing again.

The engines roared for a few minutes, and then we were off across the field, faster and faster. Out of my window I watched the starboard wheel swim up from the grass, and go on spinning round in the empty air for a little, until it quietly slid out of sight into the wing. We were away. After a few moments the second pilot passed a note back to us—the engines were very loud, and words were difficult to hear: "Jerusalem on our right in a minute—Sea of Galilee to the north." We were getting very high now as we headed for the mountains. Yes, there it lay, domes and minarets, towers and walls, and gates and cypresses, far away below, golden and purple-shadowed—Jerusalem, cradled in a hollow of the bleak hills. Beyond I could see the beginnings of the gaunt red crags of the wilderness leading away down to Jericho. Then we were passing over a black ravine as we neared the mountains of Moab, those ramparts of Palestine. A silver thread in the ravine twisted away to the north—Jordan river.

Now we were flying away from the mountains, and the waste land was opening out ahead. We were on the edge of the great desert that lies between Transjordan and Iraq. The clear light that had revealed every crag, every tree-top, in Palestine had changed; we looked down through a trembling haze as if through the slow-shifting currents of an ocean to its bed, a multicoloured ocean floor of gold and black and grey, stretching away on every side to infinity; while every now and then a small white fish drifted gently below our keel.

Things began to happen. Suddenly a feeling of dropping, followed by a severe jolt, and the hazy horizon fell away as the nose of the plane began to climb again to regain height. It had been so smooth over the mountains—where I had imagined it would, if anywhere, be rough going—that now, bucketing about over the flat desert, I felt sure something must be wrong. I must have looked panicky, for I saw the second pilot smiling as he scribbled again on his pad, and then stretched an arm back for me to read: "Always terribly bumpy over this bit—hot air over basalt—nothing to worry about." I felt much better—until I turned round in the middle of another sickening drop to see how the others were getting on, and came face to face with Jon's ghastly crocodile, which he had dropped on the floor, but which was now floating in mid-air at eye level, gazing at me with a very baleful expression as it swayed. I looked hurriedly away; my watch showed that we had been airborne only for three-quarters of an hour out of a five-hour flight. Would it ever be over?

Then Rachel, who was sitting just behind, tapped me on the shoulder. I turned, and saw that she was pointing to the far-away ground. I looked down, and saw that we were crossing a black line which ran straight as a ruler north and south. "It's the railway from the north to Mecca," she said in my ear. "It was just about here that Lawrence kept cutting it to stop the Turks using it." I forgot my qualms as I stared down at the black thread stretched over the yellow waste, and thought of the strange adventures of swift and secret daring that had been played out down there by that leader and his tribesmen.

The sun was dropping behind us when we first sighted the

outskirts of Baghdad far ahead. We had crossed the sprawling curves of the Euphrates, and were already much nearer the ground. I didn't know that all the old part of Baghdad was on the far side of the Tigris; and all I could see at first were disappointing huddles of shacks and railway lines. Then everything began tipping and whirling past the window, and I shut my eyes; when I opened them we were on an even keel, nearly down, tearing past some white buildings, and then bouncing gently along the blessed ground.

It was over—and here we were, strolling across the short grass, a soft wind blowing, to the Airport building. Jon was very cheerful after a long sleep; the crocodile was tucked firmly under one arm; and he took my hand with his free one. Then we met Gabriel. He was the Expedition driver and indispensable odd-job man—he liked best to be called the Agent—but whatever he was called added up to an understatement. I had heard something of his exuberant personality already. He was a stoutly built man—a Palestinian Arab with a round brown face and a round brown nose, round protruding brown eyes, and an enormous smile. He was dressed expensively in a bright violet silk shirt; riding breeches—just too yellow, just too tight—shiny top boots and a wide soft hat pushed back on his thinly covered pate. On either fat hip wagged a revolver. He had a bit of property among the Jaffa orange-groves, and a bit of travel to his credit; for he had once been to America, and had come back with some fine traveller's tales. For it seems he had lived in New York and commuted daily to Detroit to work for Mr. Ford. "An' Mister Ford, he say to me," Gabriel told us once, "He say to me, 'Gabriel, you are a *very* good mechanical.'"

Just now he was beside himself with delight at meeting the members of the staff again; and then he was introduced to me, and I found myself hoping, as we shook hands, that Gabriel would approve of the latest addition to his beloved expedition. Immediately I was given a glimpse of his quality. "That a typewriter, Mees? Tarrible duty here on those things—here, you give it to Gabriel, quick," and he was off, the modest portable perfectly concealed behind his ample breeks as he sidled, beaming innocently, past customs officials, and round a corner of the building to slip it away into the depths of the station-waggon.

We began passport formalities, along with a crowd of people who had just got in from Damascus. The queue of tired travellers moved slowly up to the table where a little Iraqi with a melancholy air, compounded, I think, of uncertainty and pride, wrestled with the puzzling entries in each book. Gabriel bounced in again to look for me, for the others were already in the car; I was somehow still mixed up in the queue, and I pointed out my passport to him, which I could see far down in the pile on the desk. Gabriel dodged behind the desk, picked up the passports, leafed through them, extracted mine, patted the little clerk reassuringly on the cheek, whipped the rubber stamp out of his hand and smacked it down on the first empty page; handed the stamp back, patted the little man again and hustled me out of the office and into the car, followed by faint wails of protest. "That's the way to do here, Mees—I'm good fren' all these people; but they slow, very slow—send him some nice sweets tomorrow; but we got to get out to camp—long way to go still."

We drove eastwards for a minute or two, along wide, palm-bordered roads, till a line of rather fine white houses, the British Embassy among them, built high on the embankment, marked the western bank of the river. The road sloped down between two buildings, and there below lay the Tigris, huge and tawny, swirling through the gaps between the heavy pontoons of the floating bridge which stretched across to the old town. As we dropped down the stone ramp to water-level, and nosed carefully on to the rumbling, heaving bridge, old Baghdad came for the first time full into view, and at that moment I knew again the light-hearted feeling of being set free that had happened every time I crossed the Nile to reach Amarna. Here was another symbolic transition, expressing the sense of release from everything I'd known before. This experience of hanging for a moment over the waters which were running between past and future, was renewed in me as the car bumped across the long undulating bridge and approached the ramshackle pile of buildings hanging in rickety confusion over the eastern mudbanks of the Tigris.

The brown walls stood up from the murky water, softly gold where the levelling sun struck them full, deep purple where the houses turned sideways, or the narrow passage-ways and streets split the waterfront like the fissures of a crumbling cliff. The steep ramp from the bridgehead led straight into one of these ravines, and at once the river and the sunlight were lost. A few yards ahead the main street of Baghdad—New Street, which had been made by the Turks—cut across our path. It runs north and south, parallel to the river. We turned right and drove out of the town south-easterly. It was getting dark now, but I could see the long, dusty road, shaking off at every twist the clustering houses and palms, winding out between the sunken, cultivated fields. Oleander bushes, still in bloom, but heavy with dust, swayed in the rising wind on either side. The road now rose to the top of an unprotected dyke; Gabriel switched on the headlights, and the gathering darkness pounced softly at the windows. We crossed a high spindly bridge, thrown across the Dyala river, which flows into the Tigris nearby. It is called the Lancashire Bridge, in memory of the many men of that regiment who fell at this spot in the advance on Baghdad in 1917.

On the further bank stood a few huts, an Arab *khan* and a small guard-house. A policeman was silhouetted in the doorway against a glow of firelight. He moved forward with his hand up to halt us, as if for some kind of inspection. Gabriel slowed to a crawl, leaned out as far as he could and shouted with enormous pomp: "It is the University of Chicago!" The policeman, who may not have known much about the University of Chicago, but clearly knew a lot about Gabriel, grinned and waved us on. A small metal signpost, caught in the headlights, pointed down the road: 'To Kut-el-Amara'—and brought a sudden memory of shocked grown-up faces reading bad war news, long ago.

Beyond this point we drove into complete emptiness. The car lights revealed nothing but a varying length of dusty, uneven road as they switched up and down on the pitching car. I became conscious somehow that the others were waiting for something, expectant of some change in the monotony; and then the car slowed, the lights swept round to the left, and the car lurched right off the road on to the desert track which would lead us to the Expedition House, fifty miles away to the north-east. I couldn't see anyone in the car, but could feel their antipathy to the desert pulling against my light-heartedness; and Hans said: "I can feel the bristles on my neck rising." I said: "This is lovely, and I'm sure I can smell the sea." Yettie said that it must have been raining, as there always seemed to be a salty tang in the air when the sand was wet. Gabriel told us that it had rained a good deal the night before. I hung out of the window to absorb all I could of that first taste of the great desert that lies between the Tigris and the Persian mountains.

The track ran between dunes and hillocks, faintly to be seen against the darkening sky, sleeping whales half-submerged in a yellow ocean—I couldn't get rid of an illusion of water all round—then up and over a gap in some ancient irrigation embankment, down into the dry canal bed, up again over the further bank. Gabriel took these hazardous switchbacks at a dead crawl, with the utmost care. But the next moment we would be racing across a hard, flat stretch towards a further tangle of dunes, pale at first in the wavering headlights until we drew near, then sharpening into blazing gold with the dramatic intensity of spotlit scenery as we passed between twin bastions of sand and dropped through a well-worn cutting into the empty dark again. There seemed to be no direction in our wanderings, as we swung in great curves to left and right. The car followed the tangled wheel-marks of countless former journeys which crossed and recrossed like railway points in the half-circle of light ahead. It was reassuring to see, every ten feet or so, a rough cone of sand about two feet high, heaped up alongside the track—obviously to mark the way. Gabriel told me that he had to renew them every summer, as they were flattened by rain and wind in a few months; he did it by putting a gang of workmen down from a lorry every few miles, to work along to the gang ahead, and then picking up the last gang in the line and leap-frogging it on past the others to the next stretch of track which needed its sand castles rebuilding.

"But why are they so close together, Gabriel? It must take a long time to do."

"Not too close when there's a sandstorm."

"Are the sandstorms very bad here, then?"

He lifted a heavy paw from the wheel, and seemed to thrust an imaginary horror away from him.

"You jus' wait and see, Mees—when it come very bad, you can't see one of these heaps when you're at the next." It was very difficult to imagine under this calm, star-filled sky.

Away ahead of us, close to the horizon, a pinprick of light gleamed, too yellow and too steady to be a star.

"There's the house," said Yettie. "There's always a light on the tower after dark when a car is still out."

"But are we nearly there?" I asked, surprised, for it didn't really seem long since we had left the road. "I thought the camp was fifty miles from Baghdad."

"Don't worry," said Hans. "That light is still something like twenty miles away—you won't feel exactly in a Baghdad suburb by the time we get there."

And so it was. We went on dipping and swerving and climbing—losing the light on the house whenever we twisted downwards; but there it would be again as we topped a rise, still remote, still tiny. Astonishment at this sensation of travelling fast and getting nowhere at all made this last lap seem very long. ("Of course we're not moving," said the Red Queen. "You have to travel *much* faster than this if you want to get anywhere in this country.")

Hans was right; I felt very far indeed from Baghdad, or for that matter from anywhere, by the time the car rounded the last dune and the lights revealed the faint outline of a long, low house, its dun-coloured walls pierced with the cheerful light that poured out through the pointed doorways at the entrance. The servants and guards and some of the staff who had arrived ahead of us were crowded at the steps in greeting—for our headlights had been seen from the tower long since. Gabriel, lacking the trump which alone could have expressed his archangelic feelings, heralded the safe arrival of the head of the expedition and his lady by an ear-splitting and unwavering fanfare on the horn, and pulled up at the steps of the house with a flourish. In the pleasant confusion of the lamplight and shadows playing over the laughing faces, dark and fair, as greetings were given, I luckily missed the ancient ritual which

41

was always performed at the return of the Master—for, as Hans set foot on the step of the house, a knife was slipped into a lamb sacrificed in his honour.

Inside the house, where a log fire was blazing in the big living-room, the new faces, combined with a faint scent of newly beeswaxed furniture, brought on a long-forgotten, but unmistakable sensation of beginning-of-term; of back-to-school blues. I was glad when it was possible to slip away and sort out my feelings along with my luggage.

Later that night I found some stairs that led up to the long, flat roof. Over one low parapet I looked down into a large square courtyard; round it ran a covered way, and in the shadow of this stood the closed doors and lighted windows of the private rooms. I turned away from those reminders of the closed, unknown personalities down there, for strangeness and tiredness were making me feel depressed. I crossed to the outer parapet, and looked out for the first time at the wasteland; and gradually the immensity of it, and the quietness, restored my happiness.

A gentle air, still faintly evocative of the salt sea, was blowing from the south; and a waning moon, rainbow circled, shone softly through a vastly high mosaic of pearl. Wherever I looked, the eye ran unhindered to the far horizon, except just to the north, where a low hill rose up against the stars. It was the buried city which had brought us to this place.

The quiet desert lay dark and damp, the flowing lines of the dunes merging and melting, lit here and there by a streak of silver where rain-water yet stood in a sated hollow. And that low hill seemed to be as much part of it, as blank and cool and impersonal. But within it I knew lay the wreckage of the works of once proud and eager men, their temples and palaces, their houses and streets and courtyards; the wreckage, too, of their own teeming skulls and clever hands.

I heard a low mutter of voices, and looking down saw two figures crouched one on either side of a small fire built in a hollow by the outer wall of the tower. They were two of the guards, huddled in dark cloaks, heads close swathed in their white *cheffiyehs*. One was blowing the fire; and as the flames rose and fell, the dark faces glowed and faded rhythmically, and the moonlight winked on their rifle-barrels. One was busy with a beaked coffee-pot, settling it to his liking in a circle of ash near the glowing coals.

The coals glow to red life and then die down; men rise from the dust, and the land is green and lively under their skill for a while; then they vanish, and the work of their hands is all blotted out, as a potter sweeps an impatient thumb through a piece of over-worked clay. And there goes the dying earth, too, spinning along between the ice ages towards its end. The same rhythm everywhere; heat and cold, rise and fall, energy and nothingness.

CHAPTER THREE

W<small>HAT WERE THE</small> events, both in the ancient past and in modern times, that had culminated in our arrival at this desolate spot; this particular pinpoint on the map, somewhere between Baghdad and the Persian mountains, surrounded by mile after mile of nameless desert? What was the city which we were digging? And how could there be an Expedition House there; how could a large staff, and all the native labourers themselves, live month after month in a wasteland where, except for an occasional fall of rain, the only signs of water were the dusty beds and banks of irrigation canals that had been bone dry since medieval times?

To get a general answer to these questions you must leave us on the threshold of our new season for a moment, and take a long journey in time and distance—6000 years in time; in distance, south-easterly, about 200 miles.

The time is about 4000 B.C.; the place the head of the Persian Gulf. The map (page 186) shows how the Tigris and Euphrates, which converge to within twenty miles of each other in the north near Baghdad and then separate, run close together again down in the south, before spilling into the Gulf. To the east, not far away, loom the Persian highlands; to the west the dry desert stretches away unbroken towards Arabia. In the remote past the waters of the Gulf spread much further inland than today. But gradually the silt carried down from the mountains and along the two great rivers formed a great bar across the sluggish waters, somewhere about where Basra now stands; and then began to pile up behind this barrier, forming a great delta of marshy ground of incredible fertility. Inevitably, the nomads of the desert lands to west and north, and the mountaineers from the east, all in their different ways struggling for a precarious living, began to penetrate the teeming swamp as it gradually dried up, to build first reed huts and then mud-brick dwellings in this place, where the blessed sound of running water was never stilled and where the grain grew long and heavy. It was the very beginning of the Sumerian civilisation.

Before historical times—that is to say, before about 3000 B.C.—when we know, from lists drawn up in later times, the names of the kings who began to rule about then, three distinct cultural strains appeared in Sumer, one after the other. These three prehistoric peoples, recognised by the differing work of their hands which archaeologists have found, have been designated by the names of the sites in Mesopotamia where the evidence of their existence was first discovered. The earliest was a Late Stone Age people; and because their distinctive—and beautiful—pottery and flint tools and clay sickles first came to light at a small settlement called Al 'Ubaid, near Ur, close to the ancient coastline, their remains, wherever found—and they are found very far from here, in northern Iraq and even Syria— are referred to as belonging to the Al 'Ubaid period. They probably came originally from the uplands of south-west Persia; and they may have settled in the marshy delta of Mesopotamia before 4000 B.C.

The next settlers belong to what is known as the Uruk period, because in the same way, the traces of these people, who worked in metal and built complicated brick buildings, and knew the potter's wheel, had first been found at Uruk, which is the Bibical Erech. The remains of the latest prehistoric settlers in Sumer were first discovered in a small mound near Babylon named Jemdet Nasr, and the period of their survival is therefore so named. With them arrived a very important innovation—the first beginnings of a form of writing on clay tablets.

At first the early settlers kept close to the life-giving water of the marshland streams, and along the rivers; but as their numbers multiplied, so their skill grew. They learned to dig and maintain a network of irrigation canals, diverting the rich river-water wherever they needed it to reclaim the desert land and make it fruitful. Now they could live at a distance from the rivers; and because these considerable works needed combined effort to keep them in order and regulate their use, the scattered families and clans began to draw together into village settlements, each in the midst of fruitful fields and grazing-land.

Yet this organised prosperity soon brought new problems, as the villages grew larger and the lands which they owned spread further; neighbouring territories came nearer and finally touched; and there were constant border incidents. Quarrels flared up into outright wars over the burning questions of land rights and water rights, and the village settlements began to be encircled with defences, and so became walled cities. In such chancy times, it was good for the herdsman and farmer and canal-worker to know that as night fell he could make for his armed homestead and sleep behind stout walls. The land had become a vast fertile plain—the plain of Shinar—dotted all over with walled cities, each dominating its own rich fields and waterways, jealous of its rights, constantly on the watch for violation of its property; developing, inevitably, warlike means of survival. Each town had its princely governor, its local god, its form of worship. Sometimes one king and his near descendants, of particular strength and aggressiveness, arose, and for a while their own city-state would hold dominion over many others, whose kings would then become vassal kings to the great overlord.

This phase, which persisted from about 3000 B.C. for 600 years or so, marks the dawn of historical Sumer, and is known as the Early Dynastic Period, as the power of different reigning families waxed and waned, a power which came first to one and then another city-state. Ur was one to hold such a dominant position.

The writing of the Sumerian language on clay tablets was now fully developed, as the need for careful records grew along with the increasing complexity of government and business and foreign trade. For trade in woven materials and metals and grain was now active, and gradually extended as far west as Egypt and as far east as the Indus Valley. Incidentally, their numeral system was based on a unit of sixty, an arrangement which survives to this day in our own division of the clock into sixty seconds to the minute and sixty minutes to the hour. Odd to think, for instance, that it was the ancient Sumerians who decided the way in which Roger Bannister's mile was reckoned.

It was a time of great prosperity and power, yet marred by the constant outbreak of internal warfare. And as the little armies of Sumer marched and countermarched against each other, with their ass-drawn chariots, their ranks of infantry in leather helmets and sheepskin kilts, some with battle-axes and maces, some with spears, a storm was gathering to the north which, when it broke, put an end for 200 years to these rival struggles. This was an overwhelming invasion by a Semitic people, hitherto nomadic, known as Akkadians, who were beginning to settle along the Euphrates. For suddenly, about 2400 B.C., a great chieftain rose among them, the great Sargon of Akkad; and under his leadership the undisciplined Akkadians were welded into effective troops and swept down upon the Sumerian cities.

It was a strange conquest. Sumer had to submit and become part of a vast nation ruled by Sargon and his immediate descendants, a nation which stretched from Persia to the Mediterranean, and northward as far as Asia Minor. But in time the wandering Akkadians, now settled in Sumerian towns, and mingling with their one-time foes, forgot the stormy ways of war, and were eager to learn from the conquered their highly developed arts. Until the conquest, the Akkadians could not write; they learned to do so from the Sumerians, writing their own language with cuneiform signs. The two races dwelt side by side. Gradually the power of the Semitic overlords weakened—gradually the old Sumerian strength reasserted itself. Finally the ancient city of Ur emerged once again to assume the leadership of the vast combined nation, which was now known as Sumer and Akkad. For about the last century of the third millennium—roughly from 2100 to 2000 B.C.—the kings of the great Third Dynasty of Ur ruled supreme, wielding immense power over all the land. Once again the vassal kings of the city-states looked southward for their overlord, to Ur.

. . . . . .

As the great mass of documents, in the form of clay tablets, gradually came to light in modern times through scientific excavation of ancient sites, and began to reveal the history of Sumer to the scholars who had discovered how to read them, it was possible to identify many of the places they mentioned with the visible remains in Mesopotamia; among many others, for instance, such sites as Ur and Erech, Babylon and Kish, Assur and Nimrud. But, inevitably, references were made in these documents to certain city-states, some of them clearly important, up and down the land, about which the translators could learn much, except one rather crucial fact—where they were. The actual position of these cities which had once towered so proudly above their lush fields was a secret to which there seemed to be no clue. Only chance would ever reveal them.

One such important city-state was named Eshnunna. The documents gave its name, and that of its local deity, Tishpak; gave, too, the names of many of its rulers, some of them vassal kings to the great overlords at Ur, in the Third Dynasty of Ur; some of them later kings, with strange names like Ibalpel and Ibiq-Adad, who were known to be father and son. After the Elamites had swept down and finally destroyed the power of Ur about 2000 B.C., Eshnunna had battled on for its own independence until about 1800 B.C.; but then a second great Semitic leader arose, the mighty Hammurabi, warrior and lawgiver. Ruling from Babylon, this king of the Amorites first drove the marauding highland invaders back to their mountain borders, put down the cities of the plain which yet defied him, and established complete sovereignty over all the land. It was the end of Eshnunna as an important city-state; and where it had once flourished was a total mystery.

. . . . . .

One hot morning late in 1928, the English Director of the Department of Antiquities in Baghdad was working in his office in the Museum. He was worried. One or two dealers, in their little mysterious shops along New Street, had recently been found to be selling undoubted antiquities which could only have come into their hands from Arabs carrying on illicit looting of ancient sites. The digging up and selling of possibly very important objects was not by any means the only reason for his concern, although that was bad enough. The real mental torture to an archaeologist was the knowledge that day after day indiscriminate shovelling into some ancient site, for loot, would be certainly destroying for ever priceless historical information which could only be gained through expert fieldwork in the clearing and recording of ancient buildings. But there was no way of stopping this secret trade unless the site were discovered and put in the hands of an orthodox expedition.

49

An Iraqi clerk came in to tell him that a Bedawi wanted to see him. "Very well; where is he?" "Down in the courtyard, sir—I fetch him?" The Director nodded, and went over to the window. An Arab tribesman was squatting in the shade of the courtyard wall, peacefully smoking, eyes half closed against the midday glare, his white head-shawl with double twisted black head-rope framing the dark, bearded face. The Director watched the young clerk, trim in his white drill suit, beckon him inside. He stubbed out the cigarette, tucked it carefully away somewhere in the depths of a tattered brown cloak and pushed himself up on to his feet. Then he slowly bent down, picked up a dusty bundle by the wall with great care and padded towards the Museum door. (Got something to show me, the Director decided; something, he thought grimly, the dealers won't take.)

He went back to his desk and waited while the two pairs of feet tapped slowly up the stone stairs. The clerk ushered the tribesman in, and waited while he came up to the desk. He greeted the Director courteously, put down his bundle and slowly began to unknot it.

The Director waited patiently. (He'd hardly be fool enough to bring me loot—what *has* he got, I wonder?) The last knot came loose and the grimy shawl fell open. On it stood a large grey brick. The Arab picked it up carefully and handed it across the desk, pointing a long finger at something on its top surface.

"Ah, yes," said the Director, taking it in his hands. It was an inscribed brick; a common enough find, for it had been the custom in ancient times for a ruler to have the bricks of his buildings stamped with an inscription.

The Arab watched him shrewdly while he was running an eye over the scratched lines of the inscription. (Allah be good to me, for I know that these people value such bricks with

50

writing on them. But you can never tell with these bricks from the sand, what is worth gold, what is worth nothing—you can never tell what these people are thinking, either. But Allah be merciful, perhaps he will give me a little money; enough for some cigarettes, perhaps even enough for a pair of shoes—if Allah wills, if Allah wills . . .)

"Where did you find this?" came suddenly, like the flick of a camel whip.

He tipped his head towards the window.

"Far, far away, Mudir; a place out in the desert—a day's journey."

"Has it a name?"

"It is called Tell Asmar."

"The Brown Mound," murmured the Director dubiously, "and nothing but brown mounds out there, wherever you look. Can you find this place again, for certain?"

"*Hadre*, Mudir—indeed I can."

The Director looked round at the young clerk, whose dark eyes were lively with interest.

"I want the car; tell Abdullah to see the petrol tank is full, and to take a spare tin, and to be ready in a few minutes."

The young man ran off.

A little later the car moved out under the arched gateway on to the dust road outside, and turned south-easterly. The Director sat by the driver; the man from the desert wedged himself between the front mudguard and bonnet in the normal carefree manner of his kind going anywhere by car, with one hand on the radiator cap for added safety.

Over the Lancashire Bridge they went, and on for a mile or two, until suddenly: "Huh! huh!" cried the Arab, jerking his chin with jutting beard to the left. They swung on to the true desert—there were no little sand-heaps, no criss-crossing wheel-tracks to guide them then. On that day their own tyres printed the first of countless journeys. But the Arab never hesitated as they went deeper and deeper into the wasteland. "Huh! huh!"—and the beard waved the driver to the left. "Huh! huh!"—"Right, now—to the right!" On and on and on.

After fifty miles of this, a last triumphant: "HUH!"; and close ahead of them a low brown mound rose against the sky-line.

"Here I find the brick, Mudir—here is Tell Asmar."

The Director climbed slowly out, stretched cramped limbs and looked round him. Nothing but grey-brown, dusty dunes, strewn with pebbles, empty under the tremendous sky. He walked slowly up the gentle slope of the mound to the top and began to move about it, jabbing here and there with his stick. (One loose brick is no proof, he thought.) He picked up some small pieces of broken pottery, and studied them; put a few in his pocket, tossed the others to the ground. Then he stopped, looking down at something else on the surface—a brick—but loose. He squatted down and began to brush the dust away with his hands from where it had lain. There was another brick below the surface, and beneath it he could see others—and they were holding together as they had first been built. There could be no doubt of it, here was part of a mud-brick wall in its original position. The Director took out a knife and carefully prised off the top brick; then he blew the dust gently off the surface. Yes, here it was again, the same inscription:

Ibiq-Adad Mighty King
Enlarger of Eshnunna
Beloved of Tishpak
Son of Ibalpel.

Eshnunna had been found.

· · · · · ·

"After far more than 3000 years walls had risen anew in this silent place."

Small rider at Festival.

Basket boys.

Tribesman with hawk.

The problem of excavating at Tell Asmar on a scale which would reveal the full history of ancient Eshnunna—indeed, the problem of excavating there at all—was a colossal one. No water, no house. Also, to add to the complication, the important finds turning up in the dealers' hands were traced to two mounds near the Dyala river, possibly part of the ancient city-state, but a long way from Tell Asmar; and to prevent further looting, any expedition at Tell Asmar ought to have these mounds in its concession too, so that they could be excavated and properly guarded. That would mean a big staff, and therefore a big house; everything would have to be on a scale needing a great deal of money. It was for this reason quite beyond the scope of any English archaeological body, which in those days depended mainly on small grants from museums and subscriptions from members of learned societies. The obvious solution was for the new discovery to be absorbed into the huge pattern of archaeological work being undertaken by the Oriental Institute of the University of Chicago, which was already carrying out excavations in Egypt, Palestine, Syria, Northern Iraq and Persia.

Early in 1929 letters passed swiftly between Baghdad and Chicago. Professor Breasted, immediately aware of the importance of the newly found site, decided to apply for the concession to excavate it, and so forge another great link in the chain of exploration going on all round the Near and Middle East. But he knew that much more than a great deal of money would be needed for such a site. He knew that he must have a first-class man as Field Director, one who would excel not only in field-work, but also in fitting the results of it unerringly into the shadowy framework of the remote history of Sumer; a man who combined in himself the meticulous precision of the laboratory worker with the wide vision of a great historian; and, too, he must have other than purely archaeological qualifications—he must be able to tackle the problems of administration, which in such a remote place would obviously be very formidable. And last, but not by any means least, he must be the kind of man who could handle and get the best out of staff members whose temperaments would probably be sometimes strained to clashing point by reason of the strange life they would have to lead, isolated for months on end in the desert.

Very few men could fulfil all those requirements, each of which was vitally important—and Breasted knew it. But as he pondered this problem, his thoughts turned to a dig in Egypt, which he had visited only the year before; a dig where a young Field Director—handling a staff which seemed to be on the best of terms both with him and with each other, while producing excellent results under his leadership—had already gained archaeological eminence (and a Ph.D.) with his published work on the pottery of the Ancient Near East. A man who looked far beyond the problems and significance of a single dig. An eager, genial man, with a young and brilliant wife. Yes, thought Breasted; and wrote a very long letter. . . .

Frankfort's first move, after accepting the position of Field Director of the Iraq Expedition, was to secure Seton Lloyd as his architect; and Seton's first move after that was to go and build a house at Tell Asmar. Just like that. The Baghdad contractor who was engaged to build from Seton's plans thought that if he dug deep enough at the site itself he would find water, so that he could make the bricks on the spot. He dug a well, and at 60 feet found water indeed, but so brackish that the bricks fell to pieces as soon as they were dry. The contractor nearly went mad, and had to think again. Twelve miles away to the north was the end of a modern canal. A lorry was fitted up with a huge tank and was driven to the canal with half a dozen Bedouin, armed with empty petrol tins for baling, perched along the sides. The water problem was solved, both for brickmaking and for the future needs of the expedition, except in one important respect—drinking. A sample of the canal water was sent to a doctor in Baghdad for analysis; and his verdict was unequivocal and violent, but hardly surprising, for several villages were strung along the banks of the canal; the water could perhaps be used, if very carefully filtered, for washing, he said—but it could be boiled until the bottom fell out of the kettle, and still be undrinkable. The only possibility was to have chlorinated water sent out from Baghdad—or of course there was always beer, he added kindly.

The house was built on a stretch of ground quite close to the southernmost point of the Tell, and consisted of three linked courtyards forming an L-shape; it was all at ground level, except for the tower over the car entrance, which was reached by rough wooden stairs, and which held a water-tank where the pumped-up water was first filtered. At the corner of the tower a thin pole, carrying the electric lamp at the very top, shot up another fifteen feet or so. The courtyard below the tower housed a Delco plant for generating electricity, a laundry, the servants' quarters and enough garage space for three cars. The courtyard next to this contained the drawing office, a laboratory, the darkroom and a very long room full of benches for working on the finds when they came down from the dig, and shelves for storing them. The largest of the courtyards consisted, on three sides, of the bed sitting-rooms of the staff, and an office with a small reference library; on the western side was the long living-room with its open fire and comfortable chairs; and, reached through double swing doors, the dining-room.

After far more than 3000 years, walls had risen anew in this silent place; doors opened and shut; footsteps went busily or leisurely again over paved floors; and voices sounded in the dry, clear air.

·   ·   ·   ·   ·   ·

I discovered that the name of the philologist whom everybody called Jake was really Thorkild Jacobsen. He was a Dane, whose wife Rigmor did all the dig photography. Hans had a rule that wives could come out to the dig only if they took on a real job—the harmony of many a dig has been wrecked by passengers, of both sexes—so Rigmor did some intensive training in Denmark, and emerged as a first-class photographer. The very contrast of their looks and ways, far from making them seem a strangely assorted couple, somehow emphasised their complete interdependence. Jake was a tall young man, stooping a little, as if perpetually eager to catch the remarks of average-sized folk; he had a calm brow, always in the shadow of a breaking wave of primrose hair; deep-set grey eyes, usually as thoughtful as a monk's, yet often lost in laughter; a gentle mouth, capable of setting into very obstinate lines above a heavy jaw, and almost invariably drawing at a curly Scandinavian pipe.

His special work, of course, was the interpretation of all the inscriptions found on the dig. Every evening Jake retired to a tiny room to work over the heavy little clay tablets, patiently unravelling the records of law-suits and commerce which had once meant triumph or disaster to anxious litigants and merchants 4000 years ago. His feeling for the niceties of language carried across the ages to his study of modern dialect—for I used to notice that he would refer to the 'autumn', for instance, if he were talking to me, but it would be carefully changed to the 'fall' if his listener were American.

Rigmor was as dark and vivacious as Jake was fair and quiet. Fine hazel eyes wide set beneath winging brows in a clear brown face; and her movements were swift and lithe. One seldom had a chance of watching her face in repose. I like looking at a face when the mind has drifted away from its window and is turned inward; so that the complex personality does nothing to confuse the sheer form that is sometimes all one wants to observe. But Rigmor was never abstracted; she was usually sparkling; if not that, then alert. I used to take her in, much as Richard Jefferies advised people to watch birds, by never seeming to look at them, trying to make them believe you are not interested.

Her photographs of the dig and of the finds were miracles of clarity. The problems she had to solve on the dig were sometimes very difficult; perhaps two bricks nestling together at the bottom of a shadowy pit, significant only because of their iuxtaposition, had to be photographed as they lay, if a carefully revealed bit of evidence was not to go whistling down the wind. I don't think Rigmor ever failed to produce a good result in the end, whatever the cost in struggles with tripod and cloth in bleak and dusty spots, or in long and lonely hours in the cold darkroom. I don't think, either, that patience came easily to her; but she always hung on in a kind of quiet exasperation until she was satisfied with her work.

The day following our arrival, three of the American members of the staff appeared, all newcomers like myself— Dr. and Mrs. McEwan and Harold Hill. That's how they came; but it didn't seem many hours before they were Mac and Betty and Hal. They were almost the first Americans I had ever met. Mac and Betty had come for the season only, for Mac to gain experience in this kind of field-work before going on to direct a new dig in Syria. He was a large young man, looking much older than his age, which was twenty-three; sleepy-eyed, snub-nosed and slow-voiced, with an independent mind and a slow, wise-cracking humour. He was going to work chiefly with Pierre at one of the sites near the Dyala river which was now in our concession. It was called Khafaje, and Betty was going to run the small house there.

Hal was an architect, and had come as a permanent member

to share with Seton the huge work of surveying and drawing the dig at Tell Asmar, level by level. He was slight and brown and grave, with dark-shadowed eyes. It didn't take long to realise that he was immensely sensitive to the mental thermometer, so that he remained, while always charming, reserved and withdrawn unless he was with people whom he had cautiously allowed himself to believe were genuinely fond of him. Then, and only then, would the warmth of his feelings melt his air of melancholy, and he would emerge, still quiet—he never raised his voice above a low murmur; it put me in mind of a bee trapped in a matchbox—but with a glinting eye and a rippling wit. Nothing of this showed in those early days—he and the Macs had driven in the regular bus from Damascus to Baghdad through a bad sandstorm, and they were all tired. Hal looked ill, and the dust in the air had given him a dry cough.

Now I began to feel that I had taken in quite enough new people to be going on with; but everybody kept saying, "What can have happened to Gordon and Ham?" "I wonder where Ham and Gordon have got to?" After a second day of unpacking, sorting, arranging, and still feeling that everything was rather on top of me, I thankfully fell in with Rachel's suggestion for a walk up to the dig after tea; and we set off in the warm light of the setting sun. We passed the group of buildings which Seton had shown me in the London office, first on the air photograph and then on his drawing-board. I could easily recognise the two main buildings of it—the Palace and another building joined at an angle.

We reached the highest point of the low mound. It was utterly silent. As I looked eastward I thought I could see wisps of white smoke very near the horizon. Rachel looked too, and smiled her shy, kind smile. "No," she said. "Those are the snow-peaks of the Persian mountains—something like a hundred miles away—that's why they seem so low." I stared, fascinated; and could see, now that I looked carefully, a long, broken line of white peaks stretching to north and south. Some trick of atmosphere hid the range itself—just the peaks hung disembodied along the evening sky. It was strangely comforting to see the end of emptiness when I looked that way.

Then we heard voices—men talking; but there was no one to be seen anywhere. It was rather frightening; could there be men hidden in the dusty ruins about us? "I think it's those two," Rachel said, and pointed. Away to the north two tiny black specks were moving in our direction; they must have been more than a mile away. Here was another phenomenon in this strange country; I suppose it was partly the still, empty air, helped by the hard, flat sounding board of the dead ground —but their voices sounded in our ears as if they were only a few yards away.

"It's the first of the workmen, I expect," said Rachel. "They somehow get word that the new season is beginning, and just walk here from their villages somewhere over the horizon. There'll be a big crowd by tomorrow."

"Where on earth do they live here, Rachel?"

She pointed westward to the flat ground beyond the Tell, to a line of rough pits and trenches there.

"They dig holes in the ground," she said, "and roof them with matting and skins. We guarantee them water, and they bring their own food. Every fortnight after pay-day they go back to their villages for a day, and come back the following evening with more supplies." The men were nearer now, each carrying a small bundle.

We walked slowly back to the house and went to our rooms to get ready for dinner. I was impatient for the real work to begin. Everybody was immensely kind; but somehow that first glimpse of the tangled ruins had made the solid outline of the Expedition House, with its neat sterile rooms, built round and imprisoning three small square bits of the desert, seem so incongruous as to be quite unreal; and that was depressing. Incredibly remote, Seton had said with truth. But he had probably been thinking only in terms of geography when he had said that. I felt remote from the people; and rather like a new inmate of some University hostel for foreign students—myself the most foreign. Here we all were, polite acquaintances as far as I was concerned—Dutch, Russian, English, American and Danish—preparing for an efficient and scientific term's work. Would it be like this all the time? Would I ever understand what that work was all about? Would I ever feel swept along with them all in what we were doing? I looked round at my nice room with its modern furniture that would have done credit to a good hotel; with its electric reading lamp by the bed, with its gleaming wash-basin in the corner. I tried very hard to be reasonable and not hate it all, as I thought longingly of my tiny silly room at Tell el Amarna with its crazy oil lamp hung on a hook, and its tin bath on the floor.

When I had changed I went across the courtyard into the living-room, and found that the last two members of the staff—Americans—had just arrived. Gordon Loud was telling Hans and Yettie about uncomfortable adventures in a dilapidated plane from Naples which had made two rather unnerving forced landings. His companion was sitting on a table swinging his legs, and laughing with Hal and Rigmor. He had the freckled pallor and tawny brown eyes that often go with very dark red hair. He looked jumpy—perhaps it was the reaction after his horrible flight. When he saw me he slid off the table and came across to me.

"I know who *you* are," he said, with a quick smile. "But you won't know me. My name's Hamilton Darby—Ham to you. Come and have a drink, and tell me what you think of it all here." He shook hands with a firm grip and took me over to the others. The sudden warmth, unexpected and enchanting, made me want to burst into loud un-British sobs. I'd never encountered this kind of immediate easy friendliness before. Was this a normal American greeting—and if so did it mean anything, or was it blarney? Could he really be so intuitive that he knew how much I needed cheering up at that moment? Whatever it was, I felt much better; and wondered, as I sipped an outsize Martini, and listened to the laughter, and thought of the odd things I had seen and heard up on the dig that evening, whether this strange place were going to play tricks with my heart as well.

CHAPTER FOUR

ALL THE NEXT morning the desert to north and west was alive with small black figures in twos and threes, converging on the house as if drawn by a magnet. These tribesmen were desperately poor, normally barely scratching a living in their mud villages along the canals where they now led semi-settled existences; so that the prospect of solid weekly pay for four or five months of the year was golden. As the day wore on a huge semi-circle of patient squatting Bedouin formed round the front of the house, and Hans with Seton and Jake began the task of taking on the hundred or so men and boys that were needed to do the rough digging and carrying. Most of them had brought tickets showing that they had worked here the year before, and if their records were good, they were selected again.

Some of the dark faces were very fine, but nearly all were gaunt. Their clothes were in tatters, and of every description. Some wore the true Arab brown cloak belted over a dingy white robe; a few had old Army tunics buttoned over their long shirts, which must have been relics from the First World War, picked up Heaven knows where, for some were British khaki, and others Turkish grey. All the men wore the tribesman's headshawl, the *cheffiyeh*, white or brown or checked, caught round the head with the twisted black cord, and nonchalantly wound round chin and throat; and somehow the rakish set of the headropes and the folds of the *cheffiyehs* that framed the dark faces belied the scarecrow outfits, and kept for the wearers something of their tribal dignity.

When the work of selection was over, they all drifted away, the unlucky ones to trudge back all those miles to their villages. Perhaps they consoled themselves with the thought that their fellows who had been taken on were in for a hard, long and fairly comfortless spell of work, for all they would be so rich at the end of it; while they themselves could at least take things at their own time, as they went back to scraping a living off their tiny patches of onions and rice by the canal.

They dwindled away, and the hired labourers went off to the line of pits that Rachel had shown me; and with rough spades and hoes began to fit up their curious warren for the season. Soon they had cleared out the sand which had drifted into the pits during the summer; then replaced the old bits of rail and wooden joists over the tops, and covered them with matting. They piled sand over the matting to keep it in place. Small columns of blue smoke began to rise alongside the pits, from fires made of camel dung eked out with precious bits of wood, as their meal of rice and onions slowly cooked. It was a peaceful scene.

Meanwhile Gabriel had fetched an extra load of water for them, and then had put the lorry boys on to their weekly chore of watering the shrubs in the main courtyard. Eucalyptus trees and oleander bushes had been planted a year before in the centre of it and at the four corners, and were already shooting up and flourishing. The boys with brimming petrol tins slip-slopped to and fro, grinning, between the water-lorry and the little trees, and the water sank away round the grateful roots in the small dyked-up beds. I looked at the meagre green, and listened to the rustling of the long leaves, with a kind of passionate intensity; I thought I would never again take for granted green things growing abundantly in a lush rich soil.

In the afternoon Pierre and the Macs and Ham went off to open up the work at Khafaje, twenty miles away, where they stayed for a week at a time. They piled into an ancient Ford known as Toto—because Hans occasionally remarked that that was what the Khafaje staff would be coming over in. They vanished in a swirl of dust back along the track towards Baghdad. The way to Khafaje led off westwards from this track, about twelve miles away; and at the junction there was a thin stick planted on top of a dune, forlornly swaying in the desert breeze, to mark the way in bad weather. I'm sure, really, that all Toto needed was a friendly slap on the petrol tank to send it ambling off on that familiar path back to its stable at Khafaje without benefit of driver.

Gordon and I retired to the office, where he was going to show me his kind of book-keeping, which found favour with the Finance Department in Chicago and was at present an unsolved mystery here. Gordon was leaving the following day, but had come here first to discuss his season's plan of campaign with Hans. He was the Field Director at Khorsabad, 200 miles to the north, near Mosul; it also was part of the Iraq Expedition. This northern dig was concerned with a very much later period; for there Gordon was continuing the excavation of the city of the second great Sargon, the father of Sennacherib, with its palace and temples, just east of Nineveh. He ruled from 722 to 705 B.C., more than a thousand years later than the overthrow of Eshnunna. Rachel had told me that some of us would probably be going up there in the spring; she spoke of it ecstatically, as a kind of paradise on earth.

Meanwhile here was Gordon, solemnly introducing me to the adding machine. I hadn't noticed it before under its black cover in a dark corner of the office. He took the cover off, and there it crouched with bared teeth, snarling at me.

"It's a bit complicated," he said, almost apologetically. "It was really built for rupees and annas, the currency here before Iraq was a kingdom. But now it's been adapted to deal with

64

dinars and fils. All you have to remember is to press *this* button here before pulling the addition handle, and disregard the two noughts which appear on the right-hand side of the sub-total, and then press *that* button there before pulling the final-addition handle. If you *can* manage to use it successfully," he said, looking at me doubtfully, as if he thought that the English probably still did sums by notching sticks, "it will save you lots of time, because the book-keeping down here is really quite heavy."

I tried not to show that his words had thrown me into a panic, and asked bravely what dinars and fils were.

"The dinar is pegged to your English pound, and there are a thousand fils to the dinar—no other coinage, which makes it very simple. But of course we get our drafts from Chicago in dollars, so the exchange needs to be worked out—the Bank will tell you that, of course—but Hans pays for a lot of things that are sent out from England in English money, so you have to watch that too."

I thought suddenly of the haven of Mr. Ommaney's little office among the thundering glove-boxes—what *had* I let myself in for?

"Get Gabriel to give you his accounts every week—I've been talking to him about it. He doesn't spell or write at all well, but he can remember every detail if you need to ask him. He does all the personal shopping for the staff too, whenever he goes to Baghdad, as well as the Expedition things, so you have to see that you get back the money from the staff—give all of them detailed bills each month."

(Oh! Mr. Ommaney, darling.)

"I've got Gabriel's book here to show you how to sort it out," Gordon went on, with enthusiasm; this seemed to be his idea of real fun. "I do just the same thing with Aissa's book up at Khorsabad."

He was very patient, and I calmed down. For one thing, Gabriel's entries were sheer heaven. Amongst them were patches of neat clerkly items, very different from his own misspelt and laboured scrawl, and these, Gordon told me, were done by Gabriel's Uncle Alexander in Baghdad, who could sometimes be bribed into writing up the accounts for him when he was at his house. From the look of it, Gabriel must have gone through agonies when he did it himself.

'Oct. 27. 1 Box of Sweets to Chief Inspector of Police.'

Gordon said Gabriel had managed to get the new parts for the Delco through the Customs on that date—unusually quickly.

'Oct. 29. 1 Box of Cream Toffees to Commandant of Police.'

Gordon said that was the day Gabriel got the stores from London through—at unusually low charges.

There was a flavour of the Arabian nights about those entries. So it still persisted in the city of Haroun ar Rashid, this smoothing of life's hard way with comfits. And I thought of Hassan the confectioner: 'Now I will make her sweets, such sweets, ah! me, as never I made in my life before.'

By the end of the session I felt less apprehensive; and, under Gordon's watchful eye, even managed to add up a sum on the machine that came out in dinars and fils; but for some time to come I was nervous of the contraption, and felt sure that one day, if I pressed the wrong button, it would light up inside and play "The Last Rose of Summer".

The next day Gordon left for Khorsabad, neat, serious and methodical, leaving me with several outsize double-entry account books, currencies in three languages and a slight headache. There were eight of us now at Tell Asmar, with Hal in the odd position of being the only American on an American dig. As he and Ham had known each other since Harvard days, he must have wished sometimes that he had been assigned to the dig at Khafaje, where Ham and his other two compatriots were living. Now he would see them only once a week. I think both he and I felt a bit doubtful at first as to our ability to cope adequately with our respective new jobs, and so found solace in each other's company in a set-up where everybody else knew so much about it all, after the two previous seasons there.

Late that afternoon, as some of us were sitting on the steps in front of the house in the sun, Gabriel came back from Baghdad with the truck loaded down with about ten men. He blew his usual fanfare as he shot past us and disappeared under the tower into the outer courtyard, and the men on board smiled and saluted as they went bouncing by. "The Shergatis," said Hans, and he and Seton got up and followed into the courtyard.

"Shergatis?" I asked Yettie.

"Just the same as the Guftis in Egypt," she said. "They come all the way from Shergat, which is near Mosul. Shergat means the Village at Assur—it's built right up against the mound which is all that is left of ancient Assur: you'll see it when we go north. They're skilled excavators, like the Guftis; and in the same way they are employed by digs all over Iraq. Of course, they get much higher pay than the locals; very few of the locals would be allowed anywhere near the actual wall of an ancient building with his hoe."

The Shergatis came back through the archway on foot, and made courteous greetings to Yettie. With their clean white *cheffiyehs* and robes, and jet-black over-cloaks, they were much more impressive-looking than the poor southern tribesmen. They had strong shoes and leather belts and pouches. They moved away to their quarters near the stables. "We begin digging tomorrow morning," said Hans.

The Shergatis couldn't read or write, but some of them were

full of intelligence, and all of them were full of guile. Seton told me that he once took a publication about another distant excavation up to the dig to compare a building which he was investigating with a plan in it. A sudden breeze whipped away a page, and one of the older Shergatis went to pick it up. Seton watched him studying it very carefully as he slowly brought it back. It was a blacked-in ground plan of a Temple; and to the unpractised eye, one Temple in ancient Sumer is not unlike another.

"I know this building," the Shergati told Seton. "I worked in it for the Mudir Chiera up near Kirkuk when I was a lad—here, in this room; and I remember these niches over here; and the buttress *here*." He was perfectly right—it was that same Temple; and although it was years ago, and he need have known no more of it than the particular walls and angles which he had been set to trace, he had not only taken in the whole plan of the original walls at the time, but recognised them, years later, in a form entirely unfamiliar to him: the tiny reproduction on the printed page.

As for guile . . . every season we paid them enough for the journey to and from Shergat, part of which was done by train; for the railway then extended only about 150 miles north of Baghdad. It wasn't until I had paid them for the last time when the dig was closing down in 1937 that Gabriel came clean. I suppose he hadn't dared tell us before.

"You think they waste that money on train tickets, Mees? They Shergatis? Not them. They hide in the cattle-yard at the ver' end of the station in Baghdad. Then the train begin to move, ver' slow, and—queek! before stationmaster can stop them they run fast and jump in the end truck." It was a pleasant picture; the normally staid Shergatis giggling behind their cattle-fence—then the wild rush, the scramble into the truck with hitched-up skirts, the frantic little townee stationmaster

Jake and Seton uncover the Pivot Stone.

Hans excavating.

" . . . bewildering confusion of
dun-coloured ugliness."

Hans sorting finds.

Yettie and Jon excavating.

jumping up and down on the platform calling down the wrath of Allah on their impudent heads—those same Shergatis who a few hours before had received their travel allowances so gratefully, so courteously, with downcast eyes as they bowed themselves out, and now gaily trundling off towards their northern home-town, wagging derisive beards over the top of the goods-truck at the discomfited official.

The dig began at seven the next morning; and at nine Seton came down from the Tell for breakfast, and said that in spite of four jerseys the cold wind had nearly cut him in half, and that most of the smaller basket-boys had been in tears until the sun was well up, because the ground was so cold to their bare feet. Hans said that the work had better begin an hour later; the winter cold had come early.

In the afternoon I took Jon for a walk up to the dig while Yettie went to her room to do some reading. Much of her time was taken up with looking after the little boy, running the house and keeping the stores in order (not to mention the tough kitchen staff as well, who needed it; they were inclined to gang up on the Assyrian cook, a nervous old gentleman who went in fear of ending up as a Christian martyr every time he turned his back on them to attend to the soup). Yettie did all this very efficiently because she was many-sided, able to turn her hand to anything practical when she had a mind to. In a way, her practical bent was a misfortune from her point of view, because all her inclination was towards the realm of the intellect; so that for her, life in camp was a perpetual struggle to get through the necessary chores in order to have time for her main concern. When intellectual people are hopelessly unpractical they can count themselves lucky, in a sense, because nobody makes any practical demands on them. They have all the time in the world to sit and speculate on the why of it all, while their earthier fellows are busily getting on with the how.

But Yettie could do incredibly skilful work on the dig, in salvaging and restoring fragile objects—I'd seen some of her achievements already in the Amarna section of the Cairo Museum; she could cope with any of the unpredictable happenings that crop up on a dig over and above the normal routine, whether it was a sudden invasion of our solitude by visitors, or a new branch of the expedition that had to be organised, or, once, a workman with a broken arm, for which she expertly improvised a splint until he could be got away to the hospital. Small wonder that she could find little time for study.

Hans was fiercely in sympathy with her over this problem; for with him, too, the things of the mind came first; and her wide reading and deep thinking gave him at once a stimulus and a testing-ground for his own inspiration, when the evidence of the field work, both here and all over the Near East, set his brilliant mind afire with new ideas about the ancient civilisation which was his preoccupation: its art, its thought, its religion. Like a smith, he brought those ideas, molten-glowing and still pliant, to the cool anvil of her judgment, and there, between hammer and anvil, sparks flying, the newly-created thing took shape, always well-wrought, always of high worth, later on perhaps to take outward form as a new book which would be an event in the world of archaeology.

Temperamentally they were poles apart. Paradoxically, they seemed to me the most strongly distinct personalities that I had ever known, and at the same time so perfectly attuned that one never thought of either without the other.

Meanwhile here was I, hand in hand with their son, as we toddled off to the dig, talking happily of this and that. Like many small bright ones without enough words on board yet to express their crowding thoughts, he had, just now, a slight stammer. As we reached the first slope of the Tell, the workmen and basket-boys paused in their work to gaze at him with deep interest and pleasure. "The Walad—the son of the Mudir. Allah be praised! Allah is good!" If he had been a small girl they would scarcely have thrown him a glance.

We were near the part of the dig where the Palace lay. Dust was rising from below ground level. A good way beyond it, and on the highest point of the Tell, another ant-heap was stirring; the figures of basket-boys ran to and fro up there against the sky-line. I knew that Jake was up there, initiating Hal into his new work. Together they were going to untangle the area where all the private houses of Eshnunna had been built, north of the Palace.

I realised at once that the dig was no place for Jon on a windy day. Choking dust flew everywhere, and of course the place was dangerously pitted and trenched. I thought he would be disappointed when I said that we weren't going any further. But Jon settled matters by sitting down on the stony sand with his back to the dig and beginning to sing a small Dutch song. Then he found a large beetle walking along, and his day was made—all animals enchanted him.

"Will you be all right for a minute, Jon?" I asked. "I just want to go and look down into the dig."

"You go along," he said, beaming, "and," he added slowly, so as to be sure of getting the splendid new word quite right, "*inthemeantime* I will stay here and play with my b-big, b-black b-beetle."

I went on a little way and came to the brink, and looked down at the dig, which was quite twenty feet deep here. I saw a tangle of thick walls running at all angles, and narrow canyons; meaningless tunnellings into the rubble, and twisted paths; in one place a series of five white steps leading nowhere, perched high and dry on a mud-brick platform; a pottery drain snaking round a corner. It was a bewildering confusion of dun-coloured ugliness. Basket-boys pattered up and down a beaten-earth ramp, swiftly as they went down with empty baskets swinging, slowly as they came up laden, to wind away towards the dump, where they pitched the earth into tip-trucks running on narrow rails away from the dig. I followed round the edge of the dig until I could see where the main work was going on; Seton was down there watching two Shergatis tapping along the base of a wall with their small picks. Locals were swiftly hoeing up rubble into the baskets. The endless line of boys wove an intricate pattern as they dodged in and out of the crazy passages. Seton looked round and came through the labyrinth towards me.

"Come down and look at it near to," he said, looking up and shading his eyes from the sun.

"I can't now," I said. "I have Jon up here. I just came to look for a moment this time. I can't make head or tail of it—I don't see any proper bricks anywhere. It looks as if you were just chopping shapes out of hard mud."

He grinned. "I warned you. You'll get used to it."

"What's this part of the building, Seton? It doesn't look nearly so neat as the picture in the air photo."

"I'm standing in the Main Court of the Palace of the Governors of Eshnunna—but we're going on now with what we think may be a Temple over there to the east; we finished this building last year. From where you're standing you can see the remains of seven Palace buildings."

I stared disbelievingly across the corner of my small cliff down at a wall-face running at right angles to it a few feet away, where he was pointing.

"Can you see that very thin layer of bricks right at the top, at ground level?"

I said cautiously I could.

"Ibiq-Adad II," Seton said. "Overthrown by Hammurabi—about 1800 B.C. The line of bricks below that belongs to his father's time, Ibalpel. Then that stretch of wall below it goes down to the next floor-level—*there*."

I had been able to make out the thin bricks he had shown me; but now I was lost; there was nothing but blank wall below.

"How can you tell there is a floor-level there?" I asked. "There's nothing whatever to prove it."

Hans had come round a corner below, and was standing by Seton. He was wearing goggles to protect his eyes from the flying dust, and a dark green Dutch military overcoat.

"Nothing to prove it, woman?" he cried. "Look at *that*— what do you think that is?"

He lifted his stick and touched something projecting from the wall just above his head. The sharp edge of a flat white paving-stone stuck out an inch or so from the wall; and above it the wall seemed to be cut back into a shallow recess.

"That's part of the doorsill of the building," he said, "with the door-niche above it. Beautiful. Almost certainly Dadusha. And here," the end of the stick dropped three feet or so, and moved along a clear line of paving-stones. . . .

"Don't tell me," I said. "Let me try and guess. It's a floor level."

"She mocks us," said Hans sadly.

But I was beginning to see. It was very complicated, and very wonderful. Seton had felt his way down, through ton after ton of hard-packed mud-brick walls and fallen rubble, deeper and deeper, yet losing nothing essential as he went; the evidence of each building period delicately disentangled and left hanging, unharmed by pick or hoe; subtle clues in a colossal detective story. It was a revelation to me, who so far had seen only the comparatively simple one-period city at Tell el Amarna. This kind of thing showed clearly how someone digging ruthlessly for loot could destroy at one careless blow all remaining evidence of an ancient building.

"That paving is probably Urninmar's building," Hans went on. "And look at this." Beneath the sharply clear line of paving-stones which I had succeeded in spotting, the plaster on the wall was darkened in patches. "What do you make of that?"

"Nothing," I said. And then I thought again, and ventured, "Could it be fire?"

"Not only could be, but was," he replied. "Which is why we feel sure that the floor below is Bilalama. And of course that would mean Kirikiri below that." He indicated another clearly marked doorsill, near the foot of the wall.

I pondered this remark, and made really nothing of it this time. I liked the 'of course'. It occurred to me that it was a good moment to take Jon home to tea, and I said so. They laughed, and went back through the maze of rubble-heaps towards the other building.

"My b-beetle is coming with me for a visit, he is," said Jon when I reached him. His hands were carefully cupped round his new friend. We began to amble back to the house in the warm afternoon sun. "What shall I call him?"

"Kirikiri is a nice name," I said, thinking how pleasant it was to be having a conversation comfortably within one's depth.

"Yes," said Jon. "Kiri-k-kiri. A *very* nice name it is."

·   ·   ·   ·   ·

A few objects came down from the dig that first evening; and I went and sat by Rachel in the long antiquity room while she registered them, to see how it was done. Hans had said that there would probably be need of two people at it when the dig was in full swing. She had a huge register made in duplicate with a carbon, like an invoice-book, the top sheet perforated at the edge so that it could be torn out. It was a practical idea, as it meant that the heavy book could be left here in the summer, and the top sheets only taken to London for the publication work there.

Rachel was entering a little clay figure of a man with a pointed cap, and with flattened clay pellets for eyes. He was holding a small animal in his hands.

"Perhaps a god or a worshipper," she said, making a quick sketch, and then reaching for a small pair of calipers. "6·3 by 3·1 centimetres," she murmured. Then she looked over at the box that the mannikin had travelled in from the dig. Seton had written on the lid.

"17 O–30—that's the courtyard of Seton's building," she said, as she entered all these facts in the various columns; and picked up the next object—a small clay animal. "O–30 of course is the square; the whole dig is covered by a grid system, letters one way, numbers the other; and the courtyard is the seventeenth room cleared in that square. Would you like to label the little figurine? He is As. 32/1; that's to say the first object found at Asmar, season 1932."

I made out a label and tied it round his neck.

Rachel had a comforting way, I had already discovered, of listening to and answering elementary questions without making one feel ignorant. This seemed a good moment to find out a few things.

"Rachel," I began, measuring the little animal for her. "(He's 3·2 by 3, by the way)—how can Hans say 'Here are marks of a fire, therefore it is probably Bilalama below that, and Kirikiri below that'? How does he know people's names without any inscription?—what has the fire to do with it?"

"The texts have given the outline of a good deal of the history," she said. "And as the actual buildings are dug he tries to relate what he finds with what he already knows; occasionally getting outright proof that he is on the right track by finding an inscribed brick or some other inscription of some kind. Some of the remains are so confused that the names given to the various levels are very tentative; it turns into a sort of hopeful blind-man's-buff—'This *ought* to be Dadusha's building, because we *know* the one above is Ibalpel because of the inscribed bricks, and we know from the texts that Dadusha was Ibalpel's father'—that sort of thing."

"Yes, I see," I said, holding up a long, beautifully shaped, tawny-red bead against the lamp which hung down over the bench. The bead lit up, the colour of old Burgundy.

"That's carnelian—isn't it lovely?" said Rachel.

"Lovely," I answered, handing it over. "About that fire——"

She laughed. "Well, to begin a bit earlier. You know Eshnunna was a vassal city to the overlords of the Third Dynasty of Ur. But Ur was overthrown by the Elamites at last, roughly about 2000 B.C. The last king of Ur was Ibisin, and before him Gimilsin, and both of them were acknowledged as overlords by the local contemporary rulers *here*: Ilushuilia and his father Ituria. But the interesting thing is that soon after Ur fell, the ruler here had a name which looks as if he himself came from the highlands of Elam—Kirikiri. It's possible that Eshnunna had rebelled against Ur and had helped the Elamites to destroy it, in the hope of future independence; but instead was saddled with nothing better for its pains than a new, foreign overlord. Or, of course, it *may* have been that Eshnunna was perfectly loyal to Ur, and went down fighting in the same cause, Kirikiri being perhaps a victorious Elamite general who was given Eshnunna as his share of the spoil. We know that his son, Bilalama, also ruled here; and we know that after that there was a renewed Sumerian struggle to throw out the Elamites, and in the course of this fighting much of Eshnunna was destroyed."

"By fire?" I asked.

"Yes," she said; "there are signs of it right across the Palace; it must have been a huge conflagration, as it was meant to wipe the place right out. It fits in exactly on the dig with where you would expect it from the texts, for the building level above the signs of burning is very likely the time of Urninmar, who is known to have ruled just after Eshnunna was freed from Elamite rule."

I thought of the smudged wall I had first looked at so uncomprehendingly, the clean line of paving-stones above it, and all those other fragile bits of evidence above them, right up to the modern ground level.

"After the fire," I asked, "were those later rulers independent?"

"Yes," she said. "Ur had gone down, and the Elamites had retreated; and Eshnunna went on for perhaps another two hundred years as an independent city-state until the coming of Hammurabi; but he put an end to her story, as far as we know it."

We put away the first few objects on the shelves, and Rachel closed her book. We walked to the door, and switched off the light.

"Whose building is it joined to the Palace, that they think may be a Temple, Rachel? Are there any clues there?"

"Several of the rulers had a hand in it, but it seems to have been begun earlier than the earliest Palace, and then given up for some reason—it's still in the anonymous stage, lacking any solid clues like inscribed bricks; perhaps we shall never know who built it."

Back in my room I tried to sort it out. It was tantalising and fascinating. 'Perhaps we shall never know who built it,' Rachel had said. Already I had forgotten my first dismay at the tangled ugliness of the excavation, simply because Rachel and Hans and Seton between them had given me this first glimpse into the meaning of it, into the intriguing methods by which the two very different approaches to archaeology—the written documents and the field work—were used together to bear on the same problem; Jake's work giving a starting-point to Seton, and then Seton's work filling out the bare framework of the texts, with the material finds.

Later I would learn how the dusty tangles at Tell Asmar would reveal not only much more of its own ancient history, not only more of the history of Sumer as a whole; but even new knowledge of the larger picture of the ancient world beyond. If we had been digging simply to confirm little more than the meagre facts already known about Eshnunna, the results would hardly have justified the huge undertaking and expense. It is a point that is worth making, because some people who know little or nothing about the real aims of archaeology —but who do not, for that reason, one notices, withhold their criticism about the effort and the money expended ('Why not give all that money to hospitals, my dear? So much more important') are misled into thinking that each excavation is an isolated unit, interesting possibly to the fanatic excavators on the spot, but with no bearing on another age or place.

The good archaeologist never digs any particular site as an isolated unit. I found myself musing that the man of today finding and digging an ancient Sumerian city might be likened to a man of the future, 5000 years hence, wanting passionately to learn all he can, for instance, about the long history of an ancient country called England, all he can about her guessed-at connections with other nations; and this man has had the good fortune to decipher a list of the Hanoverian kings, and come across a clue as to the whereabouts of Windsor. Digging down through that great mound, he will learn far more than the story of the royal people themselves who ruled there, and of their buildings. Perhaps he will find fragmentary documents to prove ancient links with a remote land called India; perhaps an earlier text showing that colonists far overseas to the west are fighting for their independence. Earlier still, another ruler—

difficult to disentangle because the first four of these kings all have the same name—is threatened from the Highlands to the north by a young Pretender, a kinsman, who is marching south to try to seize the throne. And then that man of the future, penetrating to yet deeper levels of the mound, may find traces of still earlier dynasties whose existence he had never suspected, with strange names—Stuart and Tudor, Plantagenet and Norman—traces which may yield their long-lost history, reaching away far beyond their ancient stronghold, to the man who knows how to interpret them, who wants, above all, to piece together the ancient times of the world which he himself now inhabits.

CHAPTER FIVE

A MONTH OF HARD work had gone by, and I was beginning to feel absorbed into its rhythm and movement; absorbed, and yet not fused. Seton felt sure he had reached the earliest period of the big building next the Palace, for in parts of it the Shergatis were finding that the thick walls had come to an end, with nothing but insignificant bits of haphazard building, or even untouched soil, beneath them.

Up on the Tell, Jake and Hal were slicing off the top layers, running trenches here, sinking shafts there. The hillock itself was formed out of ancient houses. Whereas the ancient rulers had had the power and the available labour to have a whole area of an ancient palace building properly levelled before they built anew, their humble subjects could do no such thing. As the houses in the town area collapsed or were pulled down, they were only roughly levelled, sometimes well above the foundations, and then the new dwellings were run up over them; with the result that the level of the town itself rose higher and higher as the centuries went by, until an actual hill had been formed, made of ancient ruined houses. In later times houses had been built down the slopes of this hill of ruins, which produced for Jake and Hal the surprising phenomenon of sometimes finding later-built houses in lower levels than much older ones up in the heart of the mound.

Quite high up they were already finding houses which were considerably older than Seton's oldest Palace level, for they could be dated to the days between 2400 and 2200, when the Akkadians dominated the land. Without any other clues—and there were plenty—the pottery would have told them that. So much is known about the different types of pottery in every ancient country now, that it is comparatively easy to date any level by the broken sherds found in it. The reason is, of course, that pottery in constant domestic use never survives for long; so that its broken fragments usually lie in the same building level where it was first fashioned. 'It come to pieces in me 'and, Mum,' I murmured irreverently to myself, as I looked at Jake's deep shafts, with bits of pottery embedded in the mud every few feet down, with neat labels hammered in beside them for guidance. How many careless little serving-maids, in every age, must have said that, or something very like it, as they faced an irate mistress; never to know how very helpful they were being to some future archaeologist.

Hans worked now with Seton, now with Jake; he was eager for Seton to finish off his present work, so that he could begin digging to the north of the Tell beyond the private houses, where he suspected that there were large buildings which might be even older than the houses.

Now that Seton had reached the lowest levels of the building, he and Hans had become convinced that it had originally been a Temple, as they had always thought probable; but the upper levels had been particularly confusing because it seemed that the later rulers had not used it as a Temple, but had run extensions of the nearby Palace over it. But now, far down, with virgin soil beneath it, the plan of a Temple was clearly revealed, with an elaborate entrance, a main courtyard with rooms all round it, and a recessed doorway leading to an inner sanctuary. Here stood an altar opposite the door, and on the altar a small pedestal for the statue of whatever god had been worshipped here. Before the altar was a raised platform with holes pierced in it leading down to a drain for drawing off the libations which were poured in front of the god. Hans believed that a building level just earlier than the time of the foreigner Kirikiri, which stretched right across the Temple from the Palace, should be assigned to a ruler known as Nurakhum. Below it, in the Temple proper, Seton had cleared the two lowest building periods, and now was at the very earliest foundations.

"They ought, at that rate, to have been built by Ilushuilia and Ituria," Hans said. "It looks as if the very earliest Temple was founded by Ituria, vassal king to Gimilsin of Ur."

It all seemed immensely speculative; the only clues those inscribed bricks of many years later, on which the whole tentative theory depended; could it really be true that those rough, crumbling walls, with here a niche, there a paving-stone, here a layer of ash, there a bit of a drain, tallied with each ruler mentioned on ancient tablets found in a different part of the land? The marks of fire half way down were an encouraging sign, to be sure, but to conclude that this marked the actual event of the Sumerian counter-attack on an Elamite-held city was surely highly tentative? And on down below the marks of fire—Bilalama here, Kirikiri there, Nurakhum below them; and now the two lowest layers of all—Ilushuilia and his father Ituria—it seemed fantastic that the field-work down through the tangle of walls could possibly have been so precise, so unerring, that it could exactly match the known names of all those ancient rulers.

Seton went on clearing the lowest level of the Temple. Two Shergatis were working down on either side of the recessed doorway which opened into the inner sanctuary. There seemed to be no difference at all in appearance between the rubble which had to be removed and the ancient wall which had to be freed. All was of the same material, dried mud—indeed, much of the rubble was the collapsed upper parts of the same walls— and in the thousands of years that the wind and rain had been at work there, the walls and the fallen rubble had become fused into one indistinguishable mass. But the Shergatis had developed an extraordinary sense for what was original wall, standing as it had been built, and what was not. They seemed to carry an extra nerve in the points of their small tapping-picks, as if they were elongated fingers. Tap, tap, *flick*, went the picks, coaxingly, slidingly, insinuatingly; and the bits of rubble would flake away, revealing the true smooth wall-face, the way the clinging shell of a cooked egg lifts clean and clear away from the white. To make a mistake in wall-tracing was a shame too deep for words to the Shergati; and Seton was hard put to it once to restore the self-esteem of one who, in tracing the great outer wall of a Temple, cut through one of its mud-brick buttresses before he realised what he had done.

The two Shergatis had reached the floor level of the doorway to the shrine. Seton noticed a square construction of mud-brick at each side close to the recess which once had held the edge of the door. He told the men to go a little deeper. They each cleared a kind of shallow mud-brick box, full of dusty rubble. And there was something else—something large and hard. The two men put down their picks and began to brush off the rubble with their hands. White stone gleamed through the dust; and the Shergatis blew at the dust until they had freed the surface. In each square box lay a large circular stone about a foot in diameter; and at its centre a hollowed-out socket. Seton realised, of course, that they were the stones on which the great double doors into the sanctuary had once pivoted. But it was not this interesting architectural find that was making his heart thump as he stared down at them. It was something that circled each white stone between the circumference and the hollow socket—a long inscription, cut deep and clear.

He sent a boy up to the Tell with an urgent message for Jake, and he and Hans arrived together. Jake lifted out one of the pivot stones; he turned it this way and that for a few moments, while the others waited; and then slowly began to read, revolving the stone as he did so:

"For the divine Gimilsin, the King with a pure heart for the shepherding of the land, the strong King of Ur, his god, has Ituria, Governor of Eshnunna, his servant, built for him this house."

De profundis clamavi. . . . They must have felt, as they stood there, as though they had heard the deep, ghostly voice of Ituria himself rising up out of the ruins of his Temple, released after 4000 years of silence, as it spoke to them of his past achievement—and of their present triumph. For triumph it undoubtedly was. Jake's philology, Seton's uncanny practical genius; Hans co-ordinating the work of both into a theory which he had shepherded unerringly, down and down through every doubtful stage, towards this perfect justification of the whole. Those pivot stones proved that every building level above them had been assigned to the right ruler, that the marks of fire had indeed been caused by the rebellious Sumerians. Beyond that it showed that Ituria not only acknowledged Gimilsin of Ur indeed as his overlord, but had built and dedicated a Temple for him, the god worshipped in that Temple being the deified king himself, "the divine Gimilsin".

. . . . . .

In the evening the workmen's tickets were brought down to the house; for the next day was pay-day, and the one after that a rest day. I spent the evening working out the sum earned by each man, his normal rate swollen perhaps by extra money earned for particularly good work, or diminished by fines for bad behaviour. Some of the men kept their tickets flat and quite clean in little tins along with their cigarettes; some of them handed over indescribably crumpled and grimy bits and pieces, which I handled very reluctantly. The next morning I counted out the money which Gabriel had brought out from Baghdad the evening before, and after lunch the table with the money-bags and piles of tickets was moved out to the terrace which ran along the front of the house. All the workmen were there, sitting patiently on the ground, with three of the guards, rifles slung on shoulder, strolling about among them, chatting. The fourth stood near the table, where Hans and Seton and I had taken our places. The Shergatis squatted in a group to one side, a little aloof. Hans gave out the name on the ticket, which was echoed fortissimo by the guard, and then shouted by everybody in sight if the workman in question was slow in trotting up to the table. They all seemed to enjoy the ritual; but it was a long business, and they all had many miles of walking ahead of them before dark, and wanted to get on with it.

Hans would slip the ticket back to me, I would count the money on to it and push it across to Seton, who paid the man, handed him a fresh ticket and dropped the old one into a box, to be consumed by the merciful flames as soon as possible thereafter. Occasionally he told a man that he wouldn't get any money at all next time if the ticket was in such a state; but this would usually be greeted with an uncomprehending grin—what could be the matter with his ticket?

The crowd dwindled, and soon the desert was speckled with black dots heading for the horizon. I had noticed at the first pay-day that some of the boys carried fearsome-looking weapons in their belts. They were pear-shaped stones, bored through the centre and mounted on short, stout sticks.

"They're maces," Seton had told me. "They carry them in case any of the bigger boys or men try to rob them. They're exactly the same as the maces that the Sumerians carried in war. We often find them on the dig."

The Shergatis were paid last, and by tea-time the western desert in front of the house was empty.

"What about a ride after tea?" Seton suggested, uncoiling his long length from the table.

Now, I never was a horsewoman. Yettie had told me before we left England that riding was the best way of getting away from the house for a little and varying the monotony, so I had come out all set to ride, with a pair of smart new jodhpurs. Luckily they fitted so tightly round the leg that it stopped my knees knocking when I first saw the mounts that tittupped sideways out of the stable, led by a Syce. All I had done in the past was to hack about the English countryside on an amiable, well-mannered pony in company with others, being given an occasional "'Eels down, helbows hin, Miss" as an accompaniment to a gentle canter over soft turf. Lots of people are under the impression that this is riding, and that if they can do this, they are in control. At least I never made this mistake; I knew that when I touched my mount with my heels and, with apparent docility, it shambled into a trot, it was really only doing it because Charlie and Star and Boy, just ahead, were shambling into a trot too, and it didn't want to miss the end of the funny story Charlie was telling. Someone once said to me: 'Always let your mount know from the start who is master,' but I found that I never had to go to the trouble of imparting this information—we both knew.

Yettie and Rigmor and Seton all owned their own steeds, and very pretty they were; there was a fourth, greyish-white creature, which was used for curious chores, such as keeping communications open to Khafaje and Baghdad when heavy rains had made the desert impassable for cars. She was a mare called Hillai, and was assigned to me whenever I wanted to ride; or perhaps I should say, I was assigned to her. The only person who would ever have loved Hillai would have been

Tom Webster. She had a drooping head with heavy-lidded eyes and a faint, sardonic grin. Her legs were long and inclined to get wrapped round each other, like Tishy of long ago. She looked deceptively frail, which I found rather comforting, as I first watched the others dancing glossily round the Syce. Hillai didn't look capable of going very fast. I realised that this was a mistake soon after I had first nervously gathered up the reins and began to follow the others as they moved off. Hillai looked round at me with a steady evil stare; she could not have made her meaning clearer if she had begun singing in an Irish brogue: 'I know where I'm goin', And I know who's goin' with me. . . . .'

All was well on the outward journeys of these rides, because Hillai was lazy and brooded ominously about the stable, as she stumbled over the dunes and along ancient canal-beds after the others. All was well as long as I could keep her head pointing straight ahead, so that neither swivelling eye could catch a glimpse of the brown tower, now a tiny square nick on the skyline far away behind us. If Hillai once spotted that, the ride, as one normally interprets the word, was over. The ungainly form would wheel round, quivering, and burst appallingly into life; the long, whitish neck flattened and lengthened to an astonishing degree; the slithering hooves took fire, nobly spurning the pebbly dunes, and we seemed to sail up into the air. The movement, if only I hadn't been so terrified, was rather pleasant, really, like sitting on the back of a demented migrating swan. I am sure that if I'd ever tried to check Hillai it would have been certain death. If she had deviated suddenly from her arrow flight an inch or two either way, I should have been off on my head on the iron-hard ground. So I let reasonably well alone, and clung unashamedly to the saddle. It was very exciting, and certainly varied the monotony, as day after day I arrived back at the house from different points of the compass at ninety miles an hour. It was a consolation that at least I did find myself back at the house every time. If Hillai had taken it into her head to bolt in any other direction there was nothing to stop her for hundreds of miles, unless she had gone east, and eventually run her silly face up against the Persian mountains.

Still miraculously all in one piece on that particular evening when we had paid the workmen, I saw after sunset the cheerful prick of light far away to the south-west, which meant that the Khafaje people were coming along the track; and soon afterwards they arrived and came crowding out of the chilly evening air into the warm living-room; and there was a thrumming of greeting and talk. They had had a good week; soon they were grouped round Hans with the rest of us by the fire, listening to the story of the pivot stone.

Hans stood there, neat and short and dark, in the red Egyptian slippers which he always wore in the evening when he had changed out of dig clothes; surrounded by his staff, some still shaggy and dusty from the day's work. Most of the men were taller and heavier than he was; yet I noticed then, what I often noticed later, that his natural, quite unconscious, air of benevolent authority was so strong that one had the curious impression that he was a tall man, and that people were looking upwards when they talked to him.

His English, usually almost flawless, and full of idiom and catch-phrase—which he seized on gaily and did odd things to, to suit his whim—would become a little fantastic, with his gestures, when he was excited; sometimes unconsciously, but mostly deliberately, for the fun of it. He finished the story with a wave of the hand.

"Magnifique," said Pierre.

"Just wonderful," said Betty.

"Swell," said Ham and Mac together.

Hans looked at them, glinting. "Completely swollen," he said, and there was a great burst of laughter.

To add to the festive evening, Gabriel came in just then with the mail that he had brought from Baghdad, and Hans dealt round the longed-for letters and papers. Gabriel handed a small box to Seton and I heard him say anxiously: "Mr. Lloyd, sir, I got these in the English shop. But *ver'* sorry, sir, they only got these white ones. *Ver'* sorry, Mr. Lloyd; best I could do." He wagged his large head dolefully. They were new ping-pong balls which Seton had asked him to try and find, as we sometimes played on the dining-room table. Seton took off the lid, and there they sat, a dozen of them, gleaming white in their little cups of tissue paper.

"They're fine, Gabriel—just what I wanted; thanks."

"They *awright*, sir?"

"Yes, thanks, Gabriel; fine. Good night."

He trailed away, an odd mixture of relief and puzzlement on his enormous face. He hated getting any of his shopping wrong. I found out the reason for his bewilderment a few days later when I was disentangling his accounts for that week.

'Dec. 2. For Mr. Lloyd. 1 Dozen pink Ponk Balls.'

.   .   .   .

"Come over and hear some reccuds," said Ham after dinner that evening. "The Macs are coming too."

I accepted happily; my American education was proceeding apace, and I knew what reccuds were. Ham and Hal's sitting-room was a cheerful place to step into out of the chill courtyard which gleamed steely blue in the moonlight, that night. I was greeted by Waring's Pennsylvanians crooning 'Dancing in the Dark'. Across the way, other music came faintly from the living-room, where Hans and Yettie and Rachel were listening to 'reccuds' of a vastly different kind. Mac was sitting on the floor with a glass in his hand, and Betty was knitting in a wicker armchair. Hal pushed out a chair for me, and Ham found me a drink. Red curtains were drawn close; the oil-stove gave out a great warmth. Newly arrived copies of the *New Yorker* lay about, and there were some African marigolds in a white chunky vase on a small table. Ham had asked Gabriel to find him some flowers in Baghdad for his little party. The feel of the room was unlike anything I had ever known, in spite of its exact similarity in shape and furniture to all the other rooms round that courtyard. I suppose it simply was that these four friendly people, with their still unfamiliar accents and phraseology, with their readiness to show that they welcomed my company, had created a tiny piece of America between these four walls; a first glimpse for me of the New World in the midst of this very ancient one. We talked, while Fred Astaire was putting on his top hat and polishing his nails—and I found that they were just as ready to listen to me and my tales of life in darkest England as I to them. I found myself describing the two-hundred-year-old cottage in Hampshire where my parents lived—becoming lyrical as I explained what the Hampshire downs looked like ("Sounds like they should be called the Hampshire ups"—from Mac) and the ancient loveliness of Winchester and Romsey. Ham and Hal, being architects, knew all about Norman and Early English building in theory; it was strange to think that it was still a wonderful thing for them to see it in reality. "You'd better come and see it for yourselves," I said.

"And you must come to the States one day," said Ham. "Some of it you would hate," he added thoughtfully. "But some of it you might rather like."

The smoke-haze swayed across the room, and Waring's Pennsylvanians were dancing in the dark again. It was getting late, but the next day was a holiday, and everybody was relaxed and happy. Mac said he was 'kinda hungry', and ambled off to raid the kitchen; he came back with lots of eggs and biscuits and beer. We boiled the eggs hard in a metal bowl which Ham had put on the stove to keep the atmosphere moist. Hal, at ease among his own folk, had quite lost his habitual air of holding himself together as if to withstand the chilly air of a critical world. He told me about his father's early days in the Middle West, working with lumber teams; how one autumn day, when he happened to be in town, still a boy, he passed an open doorway of a school where boys much younger than he were sitting for an examination. He had slipped in and sat at a desk and tried to do the paper he found on it, and was overcome with shame when he realised he could not answer one question, for he had never been to school. How the master had discovered him, and had become interested, and had arranged to teach him through the long winter, when the lumber men were not working. And now he was the headmaster of the biggest school in Milwaukee. It was a wonderful story.

At last, sleepily, the party broke up. I still have that record of 'Dancing in the Dark'; to this day I only have to put it on, scratched and old as it is, wrecked with the sand of many a duststorm, to bring back in a flash the sound of those voices and laughter, the faint scent of burning paraffin, the muffled padding footsteps of the guard passing the outer window on his night rounds; to see again large Mac, cross-legged on the floor, with his good mind behind his deceptively lazy manner; gentle, dainty Betty; nut-brown Hal with his shadowed eyes and swift, shy smile; and Ham, all quicksilver in mind and movement, all gold in heart.

·   ·   ·   ·   ·   ·

The finds were beginning to stream down from the private houses. Most evenings now I joined Rachel in the antiquity room. I never knew what to expect as I opened each cardboard box, for the objects were unlike anything I had ever seen before.

Yet, coming from the houses, they had a more human content than the little clay figurines of gods and worshippers and sacrificial animals that had formed most of the objects that came from the Temple. Here were mace-heads, made 4000 years earlier than those the little basket-boys carried in their belts. Some of them were beautifully shaped and finished, like large pears, and almost coming to a point at the narrow end, like peg-tops; some were fluted, or had raised shapes round the shoulder, which must have made terrible weapons of them. Of course the wooden handles on which the mace-heads had been fixed had perished, and were never found; but it was interesting to hold them up to the light and see the spiral marks, like rifling, which had been made by the metal borer cutting its way through. The stone used was very varied; there was marble, pure white or mottled grey or pink; and black steatite and limestone of many colours, red and green and white. There were so many of them that it seemed as if every man must have carried a mace.

Then one evening I picked out from a box something that looked like a small green cotton reel; like a cotton reel, it was pierced through its vertical axis; there were marks cut into it all round the outside, and I thought I could make out a shape like a rampant animal. It was the first cylinder seal I had ever touched.

Hans was in the room, examining some of the finds. I turned the cylinder round and round, and for a moment he watched me puzzling over it.

"Look," he said, taking it out of my hand. He picked up a flat piece of green plasticine that was lying on a shelf and laid it down in front of me; then he put the cylinder down at the edge of the plasticine and very carefully and slowly pressed it down and rolled it along at the same time; it looked like a tiny garden roller trundling across a miniature lawn. Then he

Impression of the cylinder seal that had travelled from India.

Impression of a fine Akkadian cylinder seal.

Impression of the cylinder seal that led to Greece.

picked the cylinder up. I stared at the flattened path left in its wake. Along that path, which a moment before had been blank, there now appeared a frieze of tiny figures less than an inch high, standing out in clear and perfect relief.

"That's not a very good impression," Hans said. "You must watch Rigmor doing it—she gets perfect ones. She makes all the seal impressions before photographing them."

The frieze showed a lion and a horned animal on their hind legs locked in combat—a small tree filled the space between their bodies. Behind each of them stood a figure, one a man with a cap on his long curls, the other half-human with a strange head.

The craftsmanship was superb, when one considered not only the tiny scale of the scene, but that it had all been cut inside out, as it were, in order to produce a scene in raised relief when rolled over soft clay. Every muscle on the straining legs stood out in quivering tension. The attitude of the two fighting animals was very familiar: the lion with curled lashing tail and snarling mouth and raised forepaws, the horned animal facing him.

"They are exactly like heraldic supporters," I said.

"Well, this type of seal with animals fighting *is* the origin of that device," he answered. "The unicorn may even owe its existence to a horned animal like this—an ibex, perhaps—in profile with only one of its horns shown. But it's *only* the design that has found its way into Europe by odd ways, and is used there heraldically—don't make the mistake of thinking that the *meaning* here is heraldic—because it ain't."

"What *does* it mean, Hans? What sort of date?"

"It's a typical Akkadian seal—it's just been found by one of Jake's men on the floor of an Akkadian house. The Semitic Akkadians learned the art of seal-cutting from the Sumerians whom they had conquered, just as they learned to write from them; but, as you can imagine, their mentality was different, and so the seals they made were quite different, not only in technique but also in the way they would arrange a scene on a seal, and in the kind of scene they selected. This is a well-known mythological scene of a hero protecting an attacked flock. Are you interested? I will give you something to read about it."

We went round to the office with its large cupboard full of books, and he pulled out a big volume.

"It's a colossal subject," he said. "Seals not only throw an immense amount of light on artistic achievements over a period that covers about 3000 years—they were made and used continuously from somewhere about 3500 to 500 B.C.—but they open up a field of inquiry into the whole realm of ancient religious thought. Are you interested?" he asked again. "I should like that you are involved in the dig, apart from the office side—up till now you somehow are not."

The touch of the cylinder seal had set something stirring in me that I hadn't felt before on this dig. I told Hans that I would begin to read about seals; up till now, I said, I'd felt rather baffled by everything, quite apart from the fact that the office work had taken up a lot of time while I was finding my way around.

"That is rather a dull book," he said, "and the illustrations are rotten. But it will give you a start on the concrete side. Begin by learning to recognise the style of each period. Ask me anything you want to know. Of course, we shall eventually do our own publication of the seals found by this expedition, with the plates all made from Rigmor's photographs. And I want, one day, to do a book on the whole subject, quite apart from this dig. But in the meantime you get out to the dig as much as you can—every day—and ask questions. How are those damned accounts, by the way?"

"Well, they balance all right this first month, if that's what you mean."

He looked at me incredulously.

"They balance? Our accounts *balance*? Jake," he called out as we saw him passing the open doorway in search of his evening bath, "Jake, the accounts balance!"

Jake turned back, and put his gentle, smiling face, streaked with Akkadian dust, into the room. "Allah be praised!" he said, as if he were remembering that terrible train journey of the year before. "We shall be *effer* so popular in Chicago."

"The drinks shall be upon me this evening," said Hans.

. . . . . .

I began to find out about cylinder seals. I had discovered something that I now realised I had been missing on this huge dig—something small and concrete and personal which might lead me back towards the shadowy people themselves who had lived so long ago in this ancient land.

The cylinder seal was an ingenious invention of very early Sumerian times. Later, as trade routes opened up to other surrounding countries, it was found far away from Sumer, the device being adopted and used for a while in distant lands. But its origin was in Mesopotamia, being first found in the remains of the Uruk period, the second of the prehistoric cultures. These people were the first to use metal, and to fashion cutting-tools, without which, of course, a cylinder seal could not have been shaped or carved.

It was first used to seal personal property. When a jar was to be sealed, for instance, a piece of cloth was tied over the mouth with string wound round below the rim. Then the string was covered all round with a thick layer of clay, and before it hardened the owner took his personal cylinder, which he wore on a wristband or necklace, or stuck on the end of the long pin which fastened his cloak, and rolled it round the clay. It had the advantage over the stamp seal that the impression could be made continuous, as long or short as was necessary. Many of the actual clay impressions have been found, sometimes showing on the under side the clear marks of the string which the clay once covered.

After the Uruk and the Jemdet Nasr periods came the days of the early dynasties of kings, and as writing developed the seal acquired a new function; it was used as a signature to legal and commercial documents, being rolled over clay tablets below the groups of wedge-shaped Sumerian syllables. But the practical functions of cylinder seals are the least interesting things about them. It is the infinite variety of the patterns and scenes cut into them, and what they signify, that make them such a fascinating and important study. Some are inscribed, which sheds light at once on the problem of the meaning of the design. Hans showed me a photograph of a magnificent inscribed seal which had been found the year before in the Palace. It was made of lapis lazuli and had gold caps at either end, and showed a worshipper being presented by a goddess to an enthroned god. An inscribed panel behind the throne read in part: "O Tishpak, mighty King. Kirikiri, Governor of Eshnunna, has presented this seal to his son Bilalama."

The vast majority of seals are uninscribed; there was no need for what might perhaps be called a caption when the meaning was perfectly clear to the men who had had them cut and wore them. So one cannot always know, looking at a seal of, for instance, flocks leaving their byre, or of men feeding flocks, or of men ploughing, even of men sitting in a dairy shaking great jars of buttermilk, while rounds of butter dry out on a shelf over their heads, whether these represent no more than simple scenes of daily life, or whether they may have some deeper ritual meaning connected with the sacred herd of the temple. When figures of gods and goddesses appear, it may still be sometimes difficult or even impossible to interpret the scene, but there is at least no doubt that it has religious significance. And bound up with these religious scenes one finds man's eternal preoccupation with his struggle for existence in the life he knows; and beyond that, with his thoughts of death and survival, symbolised by the familiar cycle of nature—the springing corn and the harvest, linked with the god who is cut down and dies at harvest time, to rise again with the turn of the year and with the sprouting seed.

The springing corn—as I looked at these particular seals, I would sometimes find myself humming a folk song which I'd learned at my kindergarten. We stood in a circle holding hands while a few of the children acted out the song in the centre, coached by a gentle young teacher, who perhaps realised—or more probably didn't—that our shrill, gay voices, in that sunny room full of growing daffodils, were echoing the first tremendous thoughts that had rolled down all the ages of the world to our small sandalled feet:

'There were three kings came from the west,
    Their victory to try,
And they have taken a solemn oath,
    John Barleycorn should die.

They took a plough and ploughed him in,
    Laid clods upon his head;
And they have taken a solemn oath
    John Barleycorn is dead.

So there he lay for a full fortnight
    Till the dew on him did fall
Then Barleycorn sprang up again
    And that surprised them all.

There he remained till midsummer
    And looked both pale and wan
Then Barleycorn he got a beard
    And so became a man.

Then they sent men with scythes so sharp
 To cut him off at knee,
Indeed poor Johnny Barleycorn
 They served him barbarously.

O Barleycorn is the choicest grain
 That ever was sown in the lea,
So let him die, that he may live
 And cheer our hearts with glee.'

So let him die, that he may live—here on the seals I could see
the Mother Goddess, leafy stems sprouting from her shoulders,
searching for her son, the dead god, who lay in his mountain
tomb. On some seals she is shown helping him, with a hand on
his crown, or on his arm or foot, as he rises from the tomb;
while a fresh young tree springs from the side of the mountain
which has imprisoned him.

That same preoccupation with death and loss and the hope
of immortality is the theme running through the great story
of a legendary king of Erech, known as Gilgamesh. He had a
strange half-human friend, Enkidu; and together they performed great feats of strength. But Enkidu died as a punish-
ment for Gilgamesh, the gods being angered by his arrogance.
And in his desolation he set out alone to find, if he could, the
secret of immortality, saying: "I myself shall die, and shall not
I then be as Enkidu? Sorrow hath entered into my soul; because of the fear of death which hath got hold of me, do I
wander over the country." In his search he met Utanapishtim,
who told him that he could not escape death, and that he himself was the only mortal ever to gain immortality. He had been
saved through the special mercy of the gods. He told Gilgamesh
how the gods had once intended to destroy all life on earth
because it was evil, by sending a great flood to cover the face
of the earth, and how, when they found that he alone had survived by floating safely in an ark which he had built, they
granted him immortality. We know Utanapishtim by another

name as we read of him in the Book of Genesis, and as the children play on the nursery floor with little carved figures of him and his family, and his floating home.

Utanapishtim at last took pity on the anguish of Gilgamesh and told him where the plant of immortality grew on the bed of a great lake. So Gilgamesh tied weights about his neck, and bravely dived down and grasped it. All in vain—for later on in his travels he left the plant lying unguarded while he bathed in a pool, and a serpent came and devoured it. His hope of immortality had vanished for ever.

Curiously enough, considering that he is the hero of the greatest myth of these early times, Gilgamesh has never been identified for certain on the cylinder seals. It is just possible that the figures on either side of the fighting animals such as appeared on that first Akkadian seal I had touched—the human figure and the half-human—represented Gilgamesh and Enkidu, but there is nothing to prove it. There is a seal showing a figure with two heavy objects, like weights, on his shoulders—perhaps he is the hero prepared to dive for the plant. There is another with figures in a boat, one holding up a plant towards the other who is crowned—perhaps they are Gilgamesh and the immortal Utanapishtim-Noah.

. . . . .

Rachel was telling me bits of the Epic of Gilgamesh, when Hans came down one evening with the finds.

"They have found a small pot packed full of objects in one of the houses," he said. "So we will clear it down here. In the meantime," he added, handing me a pinkish limestone cylinder seal, "what do you make of that? Here's some plasticine."

I turned it round several times, spurning the plasticine. I was getting used to reading the impressions inside out. I could see a continuous line of little animals with swept-back horns. Their legs had been rendered by lines of three or four tiny holes touching each other. It was an easy one.

"Jemdet Nasr," I said.

"Right you are," said Hans. And just as I was feeling pleased with myself and my newly acquired smattering, he added: "And what else? It was found today by Hal."

I looked at his mobile face, half impatient, half amused. It was the left eyebrow that did it, I thought. It often lifted quizzically, and so lightened the expression of the other side of his face, which was set usually in more serious, sometimes even grim, lines. I pulled myself together, and the penny dropped.

"Do you mean—what is it doing in an Akkadian house?"

"Pre-cisely," he said. "It's quite unusual to find anything as early as this in an Akkadian level; it must be at least 600 years older. But of course a great many seals of hard material survive into slightly later periods, and are still used, beyond the time when they were made."

"I've a seal at home which belonged to my great-grandfather," I said. "His initials were the same as mine, so my father let me have it to use."

"And there you are," he answered. "Just the same thing. Here comes the pot."

Hal came in, followed by a young workman carefully carrying a big box. A small clay pot was lifted out and put on the bench. Dust trickled out of cracks, and then poured out as Hans gingerly lifted off a large piece of it. Odd bits of metal strips and thin rods showed in the dusty interior, and we began to ease them out one by one. A cylinder seal rolled on to the bench, but its surface was blank.

"Ha!" said Hans, as he looked at it—he was fingering a little metal rod with a splayed end. "Unfinished seal—and here a finished one of lapis lazuli—and these tools—it's a seal-cutter's equipment!"

He showed us how the rod he was holding with a cutting edge at one end was a borer, for piercing a seal vertically. It was square in section at the other end. He said this had once fitted into the wooden shaft which carried the bow-string for spinning the cutting edge. Rivet-holes are drilled in china by this method to this day.

The pot also contained several copper graving-tools, and there were beads not yet bored through.

"We will get Pierre to clean all the patina off the tools so that the cutting edges show again properly," Hans said. "This is extremely interesting."

There was something particularly appealing to me in that dusty little hoard in the pot. It was the human touch again, a voice speaking down the ages, which I only heard when I saw and felt the small personal belongings of the ancient ones. This lapis lazuli seal had been turned, hour after hour, in a warm brown hand, while the patient tool etched and scraped and dug into its surface. This borer had once bitten down into the heart of the seal, whirling round under the same clever fingers that had been at rest now for 4000 years.

While I was still looking at these things, touching them as they lay still uncleaned in the dust that had hidden them so long, Jake appeared in the doorway and came quickly over to Hans. His face, usually so calm, was full of suppressed excitement.

He just said: "Hans—look!"

He handed him another cylinder seal. There was a moment's silence, and then came the wonderful rolling Dutch swear. Then: "Rachel—look at this!"

Rachel looked, gave a small cry, and reached for a strip of plasticine. Nobody asked me to look at anything.

The small cylinder went rolling across the strip. We all stared down at a strange procession which went marching across the plasticine. An elephant, a rhinoceros and a crocodile.

"Hal," said Hans, "be a good chap and find Yettie and ask her to come."

Hal slipped off.

"Mohenjo Daro," said Jake.

"Yes," said Hans.

"The elephant's feet," said Rachel.

"Absolutely identical," said Hans.

They were all wildly excited. Completely at sea, I was at screaming point. Yettie came running in, and became wildly excited too.

Then Hans suddenly swung round and roped me in. His eyes were blazing. "Do you know what this means?" he cried. "These animals were not known in this country. This seal is almost exactly like one that has been found in India—at Mohenjo Daro. The treatment of the animals is precisely the same, the ears of the rhino, the feet of the elephant. This seal was made somewhere in the Indus Valley, and must have been brought here. It proves beyond any doubt that, well before 2000 B.C., the city of Eshnunna had connections with India."

I looked at the small dusty thing held between his finger and thumb—and then down at the table. In its short journey across the plasticine it had unrolled far more than a tiny frieze of marching animals—it had unrolled a new strip of history.

CHAPTER SIX

An enormous building was emerging to the north of the Tell, beyond the private house area. Seton had leap-frogged the mound with his men, and was now on its lowest northern slope where it gradually flattened out into the hard desert level of modern times. The building was of Akkadian date, and was so fine in proportion and planning that Hans soon decided it must be the Palace of an Akkadian prince. With its northern wall close to the great town wall, it ran roughly north and south, a huge oblong of fine walls containing complexes of apartments; while just outside its south-western corner stood the fragments of a small Akkadian Temple. The most striking feature about the Palace was the plumbing. Outside the very long eastern flank ran a narrow paved lane ending at a gateway in the town wall. It was from this lane that people had entered the Palace. Seton removed its paving-stones and found a wonderful thing below. Running almost the whole length of the lane was a huge vaulted drain, nearly a yard in height, beautifully constructed of baked bricks, with a fall on it that would have rejoiced the heart of the most pernickety Sanitary Inspector that ever inspected anything in a twentieth-century Welfare State. It sloped down steadily, and passed straight through the town gateway out into the land beyond.

At intervals five smaller drains pierced the eastern wall of the Palace and connected with the main drain at right angles; and inside the Palace, all fairly near its eastern side, were found a total of five bathrooms and six water-closets. The bathrooms were no more than ablution slabs, to be sure, but each was a carefully made brick platform covered with waterproof bitumen, and sloping down towards an opening which carried the water away. But the toilets were elaborate affairs with brick seats; and each had a large water-jar built into the brick pavement. In one or two the pottery dipper was still lying which had been used for flushing the closet. The whole arrangement, built well before 2000 B.C., not only revealed a realisation in those early days that cleanliness was an asset and hygiene an important problem to be considered and solved, but also that there was the practical knowledge and ability to achieve both with complete efficiency.

The northern part of the Palace contained the ruler's apartments; it had a small entrance hall with an ablution slab, like the cloakroom in any modern house. A visitor would pass into the large central living-room, where he would be received; on the east side of this lay the ruler's bedroom, bathroom and toilet. There was another fine series of rooms filling the southwestern corner of the Palace, the part of it nearest to the small Temple. On the other side of the Palace one made one's way through rooms fairly bristling with bathrooms, to a complex which had been the living-quarters of the ladies of the Palace. We found many beads lying on the floors of these rooms, and cosmetics carefully preserved inside mussel shells, rouge in some, and black kohl in others; this was used for making up eyebrows and eyelashes. An ivory comb lay in the corner of one room; in another the remains of what may have been a lady-like handicraft or hobby, to while away leisure hours. Little pieces of mother-of-pearl cut into different shapes lay here and there, with thin sheets of bitumen near them; and there were some pieces in which the mother-of-pearl had been pressed down, forming a gay pattern; there was a small round lid worked in this way, which may have been part of a little box to hold trinkets or ointment.

Yettie and I were busy salvaging these tiny pieces one morning so that the room could be swept clean of dust ready for Rigmor and her camera. Down on the flat ground we could see Jon on his small donkey being conducted round the outskirts of ancient Eshnunna by a trusted house-boy. Away on the south-western side of the Palace, Seton was now clearing down beneath the rooms, to see what lay beneath. A workman hacking up the floor of the most southerly room ran his pick into soft rubble, and showed Seton where the floor had subsided a little. Seton stopped him, and ran his hand through the loose dust in the shallow depression. He brought to the surface a small carnelian bead and a dull grey strip of metal. He stood up and scrutinised the piece of metal for a moment, and then sent a boy with a scribbled note to Yettie to ask if she would come over. We had just picked up the last scrap of mother-of-pearl inlay, and so we both followed the boy back to where Seton was crouching by the hole in the floor. His hand came up from the rubble, and the dust cascaded between his long fingers, and left behind on his hand a little round grey disk and a few beads.

"Would you like to investigate this?" he asked Yettie. "It's a hole made deliberately in the floor, I think—and I've found a strip of silver; I think this disk is silver too, don't you? It looks rather as if something special was hidden down here. It's just on time for the midday break, so perhaps you could do it this afternoon."

We decided that Yettie should go up immediately after lunch and begin clearing the hole in the floor, while I worked at the house until it was time to get Jon up after his rest; then she would come down and take him over, while I went on clearing the hole, if still unfinished.

I was just zipping him into his tiny windbreaker at about 2.30 when Yettie came in.

"I've got a good deal of it out," she said rapidly. "It's lovely—a hoard of jewellery. But there's still a good deal there—some of it very fragile, so go easy."

"I want to see the joolery," said Jon, who had missed none of this.

"It's too far for you," she said. "We'll stay here and play in the courtyard."

"But I *do* want to see the joolery, I do," he pleaded, his eyes enormous, his mouth drooping.

"Well——" said Yettie, who wanted to see the joolery again herself. "All right. We'll come up slowly," she said to me; "but you'd better hurry. All the things you'll need are up there."

I rushed off. It was quite a long way to reach even the southern end of the Palace. Past the stables, past the Gimilsin Temple, up the stony rise past the houses—a wave of the hand to Hal, bent over his surveying-table—down again on the far side to where the Palace lay, swarming with workmen, Seton moving among them, austere and unhurried. Beyond lay the desert; very yellow today in the afternoon sunshine, stretching away to the far northern horizon and the soft blue sky.

The hole in the floor was about two feet across, and now quite deep. All round the rim were small cardboard boxes, each holding different kinds of objects as Yettie had sorted them. I sat down on the ground and inspected them. There were wedge-shaped pieces of lovely rich blue which I knew was lapis lazuli; more wedge-shaped pieces, just the same size, of dull grey which Seton said were silver—beads of carnelian and silver and onyx, and many small round silver disks, rather like large pendants, for each had a small silver strip attached to the rim pierced as though to take several rows of threads. There were two long pins with large lapis and silver heads, and one or two lapis amulets, which looked as if they might be bulls. I thought how beautiful this combination of colour and metal must have looked when it was new and sparkling—the translucent glow of the red-gold carnelian, the rich opaque blue of the lapis, both set off with the flash and gleam of silver; not realising that later on, under the skill of Pierre's chemistry and Yettie's restoration, it would once again be seen almost as brilliant as the day it was made. Meanwhile here I was, flat on my face, gingerly brushing away the dust into a box which I had put into the hole; as it filled I lifted it out and poured the contents into a fine sieve in case something had been missed. Every time I did this, tiny beads remained on the mesh, and I wondered what they could have been used for; they were almost too small even for threading between the large ones. Then my brush encountered something solid. I blew for a few moments, and a gleam of strong blue showed through the dust. Carefully I blew again until I had cleared the whole outline. Then I slid a broad knife-blade alongside it and gradually worked it under until it was supporting the small object. I lifted it out of the hole, and cleaned it very gently with a small fine brush. It was a bird with outstretched wings, and the pointed end of one lapis wing was capped with silver. The other wing had lost its cap, but it was pierced with a small hole near the tip, clearly for some attachment. The head, too, was of silver, but it was not the head of a bird. Grey and dusty and flattened though it was through its long imprisonment, I could see that it was the head of a lion. And I could see something else: a thread of wire still passed through the silver neck and through a hole pierced in the lapis neck to join them; and on the wire was threaded one of the tiny carnelian beads I had found. The bead was simply a finishing touch to heighten the colour effect of the joined silver and lapis. It was as well that I hadn't tried to pick out the amulet with finger and thumb; the head was very loose, and the wire would probably have broken at a touch.

I looked into the box where Yettie had put all the bits of silver and discovered what I was hoping for—a small triangular piece, looking like a slightly flattened pencil case. There it was. I picked it up and slipped it on to the wing which had lost its silver cap. It fitted exactly. I knew by now from the cylinder seal designs who the amulet was. He was Imdugud, the lion-headed eagle, an emblem of a fertility god, Ninurta, a lord of plants and slayer of monsters. Then I found another smaller amulet of Imdugud; this time his head, body and tail were all of silver, and his wings alone of lapis lazuli.

Yettie and Hans arrived together, with Jon beaming between them, and Yettie took my place on the ground. Hans seized upon the amulet. Jon stood by and quietly put his hands behind his back, as he had been trained to do whenever he was near any antiquities. He was absorbed in watching the tiny fragments coming up one by one out of the hole. We all stood round as Yettie ran her brush finally round the interior of the hole.

"I think that's all," she began to say; and then: "No, here's something else at the bottom." The brush moved carefully backwards and forwards through the dust, and now we could see a circular outline.

"I want something quite flat," she said; "I don't dare lift it."

Hans broke the edge off a box lid, and handed it down to her. She laid it down close to the round object, and with infinite care prised up the edge of it with a knife and slid the piece of strong cardboard beneath it, bit by bit, brushing and blowing and coaxing the disk out of its cranny. At last she was able to bring it up to ground level, and we could see it in broad daylight for the first time. It was a magnificent ornament of silver, about five inches in diameter, with a raised boss in the centre; and even now, choked with dust though it was, we could see that between the boss and the circumference ran four concentric circles of delicate filigree work. It was a huge version of all the little disks that we had found, except that it had no attachments to the rim; clearly they all belonged together, linked by the beads and amulets; but the size and weight of the great disk showed that it could be no ordinary necklace. Hans held the large amulet of Imdugud in his hand, and turned to look across the Palace wall at the ground-level fragments of the little Temple, which was only ten yards or so distant from this point, jutting out at right angles.

"Seton," he said, "has Rigmor got all the photographs we want of the Temple as it stands?"

Seton said he had seen the developed negatives that morning, and that they were all right. A building, however fragmentary, was never demolished until the only visual records of it—the photographs—were known to be perfectly satisfactory.

"Well then," he went on, "will you begin going down there tomorrow? I very much want to know what is beneath."

"I believe we can make a wonderful restoration of this," said Yettie, looking at a deep strip of silver on her palm which had long pendants still wired to it here and there. "I can see the original arrangement of the pendants here exactly, so that we shall be able to put back some of the loose ones. Couldn't you get Pierre over to do the silver?"

"Yes—excellent," he answered. "And then you reconstruct the whole thing; and Rachel can make a full-scale painting of it."

After the following day off, when the Macs and Ham went back to Khafaje, Pierre stayed behind, and vanished from sight into his little laboratory next to the darkroom. When next we saw the hoard of jewellery, days later, the silver was shining again, and the carnelians and lapis lazuli gleamed and glowed. Now that it was clean, the big disk was found to be pierced on either side so as to take three strings of beads, and Hans thought it was most likely a ceremonial pectoral; and that the deep silver band with long pendants wired to it along one edge, was a head fillet. Yettie began with infinite patience to fit the hundreds of pieces into a coherent whole, first securing the amulets with wire and the tiny carnelians to a chain of blue beads, and filling up all the gaps along the edge of the fillet with matching pendants of silver and lapis. It took days. At last it was ready to hand over to Rachel, who was rejoicing at this welcome variant to her normal daily work; for she was a fine artist. She arranged the whole collection on a drawing-board, the head fillet at the top, then the chain of amulets, then a collar of alternate silver and lapis wedges, and then the great shining pectoral hanging between its treble row of beads. It lay there glowing; and Rachel, purring happily, settled down to make what resulted in a glorious colour reconstruction.

Meanwhile the Akkadian building of the small Temple had vanished for ever, and Seton's Shergatis were carefully tracing down into the level below. I was watching them at this task one morning when Hans, who was crouching above the trench out of which the Shergati's head emerged, suddenly said: "Here we are—planoconvex."

I had a flashback of Hampstead Tube Station, and saw myself bustling towards Fitzjohn's Avenue—could it really be only five months ago? I felt like Jon—"I want to see the plano-convex brick, I do."

"D'you see it?" Hans said to me, pointing down at the wall in the trench. "Bricks put sloping, first one way, then the other. There's a loose one—I'll get it." He removed a brick and handed it up to me. Flat on the base, and rounded on the top; smoothed off in rough ridges, as though fingers had been quickly drawn through the mud; and there were two distinct thumb marks as well. I looked at Hans.

"I know *how* they were made, and how the walls were built

with them," I said. "But what does it mean? I suppose I ought to know."

"It means," he said patiently, but looking rather as if he wondered how anyone could possibly sit for a month taking down notes about anything without knowing what it was all about—"that we have reached the Early Dynastic period. The use of these bricks coincides almost exactly with that time, from the beginning of the ruling dynasties and the time, about 600 years later, when the Akkadians overran the Sumerians. Whenever you find them you can safely say Early Dynastic. These top bricks indicate the last pure Sumerian Temple here—above it was the earliest Akkadian Temple." So that was it.

"Will you find Early Dynastic buildings under the Palace too?"

"Certain to," he said. "Although the jewellery hoard was found in an Akkadian floor, it has some features like jewellery of considerably older date; the small disks—they're spacers, really—with pieces joined on for threading to strings of beads, for instance, are just the same as some found at Ur in the Early Dynastic period."

The same evening Seton brought down the last objects which belonged to the Akkadian period of the little Temple; among them a grey stone cylinder seal. It showed two gods armed with spears attacking a terrible monster—a dragon with seven heads. The god attacking the heads had succeeded in slaying four of them, for they hung down limply, the spear-point still piercing the uppermost. But the three remaining heads were still erect and menacing, with forked tongues flickering at the god. Out of the monster's back rose long trembling flames.

Hans was intensely excited. "Slayer of monsters," he said to Rachel. "I'm wondering if this ties up with the Imdugud amu-lets in the jewellery hoard; that might be the ceremonial jewellery worn by an official of a temple dedicated to Ninurta; that corner of the Palace, so near the Temple, might be the living quarters of its officials."

"And I am wondering about Herakles," said Rachel, looking down at the seal.

"You mean the seven heads of the monster."

"Yes," Rachel answered. "And there is a second god here helping the slayer of the monster, just as Iolaus helped Herakles —and look at the flames rising from the dragon—Herakles had to use fire in the end, to vanquish the Hydra."

It was another of those exalted moments which repay days and weeks of patient routine work—when a small dusty object saved from the rubble of the dig would suddenly light up the first step of a path which had not been visible till then, but, once seen, led the way to fresh knowledge for those who knew how to follow it. I'd felt it with the others when Hans had first explained the significance of the seal from Mohenjo Daro; imagination had been sent racing then, far and far away, a thousand miles and more, watching the ancient caravans moving along routes already established in the dawn of history, all the way from the Indus Valley, bringing wares, and news of distant lands, to the citizens of Eshnunna.

And now—Rachel's words had opened up a strange new path—running this time north-westerly through Asia Minor towards Greece; a path that travelled through time as well, a thousand years of time, carrying down with it very ancient stories, half-remembered, half-dreamed, of gods who helped men by saving their flocks from savage monsters. From that first clue yielded by the little grey stone cylinder seal, Rachel began to forge, link by link, a chain of powerful evidence, which she later published, showing that Herakles, mighty hero of Greece, owed his origin to a fertility god of ancient Mesopotamia.

· · · · · ·

I was having a busman's holiday. It seemed that Pierre had decided that as there was a tame accountant roaming loose at Tell Asmar, he might as well stop wrestling with his own sums; and he sent over a message to ask Hans if I could go over one day to Khafaje and sort things out. So I set out with Gabriel very early one morning; he was going to drop me at Khafaje, pick up their shopping list and go on to Baghdad; and as all the Khafaje people were coming back that night to Tell Asmar for the weekly break, I could go back with them. Ham had also suggested a ride sometime in the afternoon, and had promised it would be a gentle one. Although I was eager to see the dig at Khafaje, I was feeling mildly put upon. I had a lot of letters to get through for Hans, and a long report of his to get typed out for Professor Breasted, who was now in Egypt. Hans' manuscripts were fascinating but painful, for they nearly always had extra bits pinned on unexpectedly here and there. Red chalk lines and arrows led accurately backwards and forwards and up and down through the clear, rushing handwriting, and always everything turned out to be present and correct, even if some of it was upside down. I would feel rather like Theseus following the scarlet thread from the depths of the labyrinth, as I sat by the typewriter, slowly revolving the manuscript in search of the end of a sentence. It took time. Why couldn't they manage their own accounts at Khafaje, for goodness' sake?

But it was difficult to grouse on such a wonderful morning. The desert was all silver and gold, for the clear air was playing tricks on us, and conjuring up great stretches of water where no water could be. I had never seen a real mirage before. Sometimes we seemed to be heading straight for a sheet of water which we never quite reached—the edge of the vast lake remained always a few feet ahead of our swift wheels. The tops of the sand-heaps which Gabriel had made to mark the track, showed up through the phantom water, black against the dazzling light, curving and curling away into the distance ahead of us, like a string of little marker-buoys bobbing on the calm surface of a summer sea.

After a while we came to the junction where a sidetrack led to Khafaje, and the car swung off to the right. Fairly soon I could see a row of palm trees hanging near the western horizon; but Gabriel said that they, too, were mirage.

"There's trees further away there awright," he said. "But much longer off—away over the river—them's just reflackshuns."

Then I saw a long bank of earth on the right, surrounded by a shining lake, and there were little black figures moving up and down it against the skyline. I'd just decided that they were imaginary too when Gabriel waved a fat hand and said, "Khafaje dig!" And at the same time the lake quietly rolled itself up and vanished. The bank—which was the dump-heap of the dig—stopped playing at islands, and came gently to rest on dry ground as we drew near.

"I take you to the house, Mees? Or you stop at the dig first? There's Mr. Delougaz—over there. An' Mr. Darby over *there*."

I hadn't seen either of them, but Gabriel had spotted them in different parts of the dig; he showed me Pierre's head, which could be seen all by itself, rather startlingly, at ground level. I said I would get out and go and look at the work; and Gabriel drove on to the house. Pierre, who had been working at the bottom of a trench, and had straightened up on hearing the car, waved as I approached.

"Pierre," I said. "I've seen a planoconvex brick!"

His round, red face twinkled into laughter. "*Tiens!* If it's deez you wish to see, you've come to a good place."

He pointed to the wall in the trench, and all around; everywhere I looked were the odd-shaped bricks, built zigzag, with a flat course between each double row.

"Early Dynastic building, of course," I said nonchalantly, tapping my jodhpurred leg with a riding-switch, and trying not to spoil it by laughing.

Pierre looked gratifyingly surprised at my vast erudition, and climbed slowly out of the trench, and we walked over to Ham, who was standing on the top of a low wall directing some workmen.

Unlike Tell Asmar, Khafaje was very flat. From the top of Ham's wall, the whole dig could be taken in like a plan drawn on paper—and across the dig, a few hundred yards away to the west, I could see the little dig house—tiny compared with the impressive proportions of the house at Tell Asmar. To the right of it, towards the north and not far distant, I could see a wonderful thing—a gleam of water: real water this time. Beyond that, on the further bank of the Dyala river, something else which brought utter refreshment to eyes grown over-accustomed to this unshaded glaring land—a dense blue-green belt of palm trees. I found it difficult to stop looking and to concentrate on the dig; but Pierre was explaining it.

"Nothing like it ever before found," he was saying. "See the curved wall there all round the platform."

"And all made of lovely planoconvex bricks," said Ham banteringly. "We've only cleaned about sixty thousand of them; I know them all like the back of my hand."

Between them they explained the extraordinary plan at our feet. Although denuded to ground level by wind and rain, enough evidence had been found to show that a Temple had been built on a great raised oblong platform with steps leading up to it from a courtyard; and this platform and courtyard had been contained by a huge oval wall, pierced at the end furthest from the Temple by a fine gateway flanked by towers. I could see the oval wall clearly; but as there was nothing to be seen within its curve except a brick plan flat on the ground, it didn't seem to me too idiotic to ask how they could possibly know that a Temple had once stood there on a raised platform. Pierre led me solemnly across precarious criss-cross paths which were the tops of walls, with pits and trenches on either side. Ham called out, "See you at lunch," and dropped out of sight into a trench. At one point we passed a great round pit empty of any walls, and Pierre said that it was one of the holes made by the robbers who had looted the site before the concession to dig here had come into our hands. We crossed the wide curved wall and walked across the courtyard towards the oblong of solid brickwork at the southern end. I could see now that although this platform was only a few courses high, it had beautifully symmetrical shallow buttresses along the sides.

Pierre stopped several feet away from the long front edge of the platform and pointed to the ground. All I could see were two rough brick steps all by themselves, quite isolated and completely unimpressive.

"Dis is how we know," he simply said.

A few weeks before I would probably have decided, with the scepticism born of sheer ignorance, that a statement like that could not possibly have any solid basis. Now I knew quite enough of the ingenuity of good field work to wait silently and sensibly while Pierre filled out this statement. The two steps, he explained, were so well preserved that the rise and tread of each could be measured accurately. So by measuring the distance between the lower step and the base of the platform, it was easy to calculate how many steps had originally led up to the top, and therefore how high this platform had once been. It worked out at about fifteen feet. I'd noticed that the steps weren't opposite the centre of the platform, but rather towards its eastern end. Pierre said that this was the strongest evidence that a Temple, and not a secular building, had once stood there. The stairs would certainly have led up immediately opposite the main doorway of any important building, and this was precisely where the main doorway of Temples on other sites had been found; in the long northern side towards the eastern end. The little Temple at Tell Asmar was found to follow just the same plan.

We went on to the far side of the courtyard where Pierre showed me rows of storerooms, which once had held the implements of war and peace within the great protecting wall. In one, more than forty mace-heads had been found the year before; in another, flint reaping-sickles with sharp saw edges, the bitumen still thick where they had been fastened into wooden handles; in yet another, a pile of clay net-sinkers with the twine of the net still to be seen knotted round a few of them. Some of the floors of these rooms had been plastered, and Pierre showed me one curiously touching sight. One day, more than 4000 years ago, while the floor of one room was still soft, a Sumerian baby had tried out its new achievement of walking, and had left a perfect footprint in the plaster—tiny rounded toes and firmly-pressed-down heel criss-crossed with a network of lines. That baby had set its small anonymous mark there hundreds of years before Abraham, away down in Ur, had gathered up his family and his belongings in the days of Hammurabi, to set out westwards for his new homeland.

We walked to the dig house. It consisted of a tiny square courtyard—almost filled with a large round flower-bed—enclosed on the two sides nearest the dig by walls, and on the two others by a series of small, cottagey rooms. The flower-bed had an attractive edging of small brown glass circles, which on closer inspection turned out to be the upturned bases of innumerable beer-bottles carefully pushed in upside down.

Betty, having arranged the lunch, was sitting in the sunny

courtyard, busily making diagram drawings of pottery with the aid of an enormous pair of calipers. A woolly old black-and-white bitch, with three puppies tumbling about her, was dozing on the ground near Betty on one side, and lazily thumped us a welcome. She was rather inappropriately called Rimush, in honour of the successor of Sargon of Akkad, a stone vase with his name inscribed on it having been found here the year before.

Quietly sitting on the ground on the other side of Betty's chair was a small, enchanting gazelle. He was completely tame, and adored going for walks with Rimush and the staff, I was told. A few tame rabbits galumphed about the courtyard—it was all very peaceful.

"Coffee," said Betty, getting up. "Lunch won't be for another hour or so. Mac's in the darkroom."

We had spent a long time ambling round the dig, and the morning was half gone.

"Accounts," I said to Pierre.

He looked at me sideways, wickedly, and then laughed.

"Dey not so bad somehow, after all—I give you perhaps one little sum, so we all feel good inside. We just think—perhaps you like a day off and see Khafaje."

For a moment I thought of my desk piled up with untyped shorthand notes for letters, and the long report as well—and could have slapped the kind little man. Then I suddenly felt in a holiday mood, especially as it was all so unexpected, when I had come intending to be quite hard at it most of the day; and decided, now that I was here, to enjoy myself thoroughly.

It was a lovely day. After lunch we sat in the sun—and out came Ham's portable gramophone; and soon the strangled, toneless, yet somehow attractive voice of Noël Coward told us that he was *sure* it was Something to do with Spring. Later I added up one small sum, as requested. Later still, Ham and I rode to the Dyala river, which flowed wide and curving between steep banks. A foot-path wound up and down along the bank, between low scrub and grass; and across the water I could see bright patches of cultivated ground, and clusters of small mud houses grouped against the lovely trees, which stretched cool and green towards the Tigris, a few miles away. Along the path we went for a long way in single file, but at last left the river where it swung away to the north; and rode more sociably, side by side now, cantering across the desert in a great circle back towards the house. Ham was a naturally good horseman, and communicated his nonchalant unnervous ease to me, so that for the first time out here I knew the joy of a long and tranquil ride with a gay and gentle companion. The west was flaming as we neared the dig, and as the sun vanished below the trees now far behind us, the desert swiftly darkened. Ham said that we had better walk the horses back the last few hundred yards, as there were several trial trenches running uncomfortably near our path.

As we slowly came near the house, I kept thinking I heard a tiny pattering behind me, and said so. Ham looked back at the already dark sand, almost black against the glowing sky, and then bent right down so that his head was almost at ground level. He laughed. "Yes, I thought so—look from down here."

I stood on my head too, and looked back. Silhouetted against the sunset was something V-shaped; small and neat and black. It was the horns of the gazelle; he had come out to meet us, and was now pattering home with us at a discreet distance from the horses' hooves.

Tea round a softly glowing oil lamp—no electricity at Khafaje—in the small, cottage-like living-room. Then they all began bringing out small cases and grips from their rooms and stowing them in Toto, which Mac had brought up to the door. Last instructions to the guards; and then we were away, heading for Tell Asmar, Pierre huddled in a fur-lined coat next to Mac, and slim Ham fitting himself in somehow between Betty and me. Soon the Tell Asmar light shone out on the horizon. My lovely day was nearly over—one of those quite simple, yet rare days, so few in a lifetime, that drop into your heart, and lodge there for ever, while a thousand others, perhaps far more eventful, go fluttering away on the wind, forgotten.

Eventually I got back to that report; and typed it out against the insistent jingle which wouldn't leave me in peace:

'It is extremely interesting to note that this jewellery was found in a building dated by other evidence to Akkadian times;'

("*A feeling I can't express,*
A sort of lilt in the air . . .")

'and yet it shows clear survivals of pre-Akkadian forms found at Ur and in the contemporary cemetery at Kish.'

("*I'm sure it's something to do with Spring!*")

.   .   .   .   .   .

Everywhere at Tell Asmar now the dig had reached down to the Early Dynastic period. Jake and Hal had unravelled a large house all of planoconvex bricks with five arched doorways, the first ever known; and in this house, too, was another unique find: a small square window with carbonised fragments of the wooden frame still clinging round the opening.

Seton had gone down below the Akkadian Palace in the large corner room where the Palace nearly touched the little Temple. One morning one of his Shergatis was in the corner of this room, tracing the wall near the angle. It had been carefully plastered—a circumstance which always made a wall easier to follow. Suddenly the point of his pick pierced the wall, and slid into it up to the haft. Drawing it out, he peered unhappily at a small round hole, framed by what looked like

The copper board when first discovered.

Drinking tube, strainer and inscribed bowls.

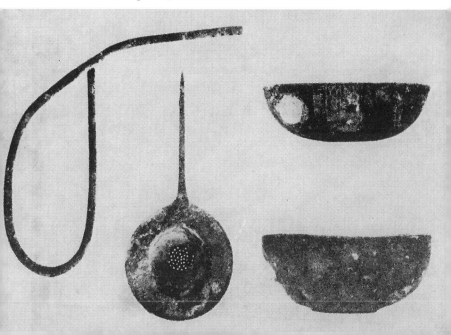

Looking south over the Akkadian Palace towards the Abu Temple.
The tower of the Expedition House can just be seen on the skyline.

Hans in the Temple with Dr. Breasted who is standing immediately
above the buried hoard of statues.

thick yellow pottery, right inside the thickness of the wall. He showed it to Seton, who dusted away the rubble from the hole, and revealed the side of a great yellow pottery vessel at least an inch thick. The pickman had inadvertently driven his pick through the side of a pot.

A large pot right inside a wall. . . . It was a strange thing; and he sent a boy to find Hans. Luckily Jon and I were walking up with him to the dig at that moment. Together he and Seton crouched in the corner and carefully cleared back the loosened rubble until there was a big cavity under the wall; but the great vessel was badly cracked, and as it slowly lost the support of the earth around it, large pieces began to break away and fall to the ground. As the dust cascaded down, following the sherds, a gleam of peacock blue and green suddenly shone out of the grey, shadowy hole. Hans got his head and shoulders under the hanging wall and had a long look.

"There are many metal vessels in here," he said, his voice muffled and excited. "And I think I can see a knife-blade—bright green—everything is heavily oxidised."

"I w-want to see the bright-green knife-blade," said Jon promptly; and Hans helped him down into the dusty trench. He went down on all fours, and would have disappeared completely into the hole under the wall if Hans had not kept a firm grip on the seat of his small trousers.

"We must get the whole of the wall away round it and from above, brick by brick," Hans said. "We can't risk it coming down on the pot suddenly; it's broken to bits, and probably everything inside is very fragile, in any case. But first I want a photograph of it like this, before we remove any more of the pot."

For the rest of that day, and all the morning of the next, the preliminary work went on—photographs, clearance; photographs, clearance. Then, when the dangerous weight of the overhanging wall had been entirely removed, Yettie took over and began getting out the contents. The pot was cram full. We took up padded boxes and boards, and as the objects were eased away from the sides of the pot we slid them first on to the boards, and then, if they did not seem dangerously fragile, lifted them by hand into the boxes. There were nests of oval copper dishes and bowls, packed one inside the other to save space; each of these nests had become stuck together into one mass, and as the metal of the dishes was thin, we wondered if they could ever be successfully disentangled. It looked like another big job for Pierre.

Even before they were treated in any way, Hans said that many were identical in shape—and therefore contemporary or near-contemporary—with the gold vessels found at Ur by Woolley in the Royal Tombs, belonging to the First Dynasty of Ur. We could see, even through the blue-green encrustation, that some of the bowls were beautifully fluted, in just the same way as some from Ur.

"I will not say anything until it has been further cleaned," said Hans at dinner that night, when all the copper objects from the pot were at last safely down at the house, "although I know what I am thinking. I've sent an S.O.S. to Pierre—he will come tomorrow—let us try not to hope too violently for an inscription."

Pierre arrived and stayed for a week, hardly stirring from the laboratory. One by one he coaxed the bowls out of their nests; one by one they lost their gleaming turquoise surface and turned a sober copper brown. At last he said he had done all he could, and the whole array was set out along the shelves of the antiquity room. It was almost impossible to believe that all these vessels had been packed in that one jar, huge though it was. There were sixty bowls; four lamps made in the shape of shells —identical, these, with those found at Ur; four strainers with long handles and neatly patterned perforations; four daggers with the silver foil which had once covered their handles still preserved, although the handles themselves, probably of wood, had perished. There was a long tube with perforations at one end—a unique find, though we knew its use at once from its appearance in certain scenes depicted on cylinder seals, where men were shown sitting on either side of a wine-jar drinking from it by means of long tubes dipped in the liquid. It was a drinking-tube: the first ever found.

There was another wonderful find. Whereas the handles were missing from the four copper knife-blades, there was one metal handle without any sign of a blade. It was wrought of bronze, that is to say, the copper had been hardened by the addition of a small percentage of tin; it had a fine openwork pattern, and a small lump of metal could be seen inside the handle, rattling about loose, too large to fall out. Pierre found something very intriguing in the slit where once the blade had been fastened to the handle—rust. That meant iron—and accounted for the fact that the blade was missing; it had simply rusted away during the thousands of years in the jar. Then Pierre extracted the small lump of metal from the handle, and analysed it as far as he could with the equipment available; and came to the conclusion, because of the lack of nickel, that the iron was terrestrial and not meteoric. Metal objects of meteoric iron were already known at this date; but if Pierre were right it was by far the earliest example ever found of an object forged from terrestrial iron—quite 1500 years earlier than the knife which was presented to Tutankhamun as a rare and costly gift by a Hittite prince, and until this moment the earliest known. Later in the year this iron was sent to the National Physical Laboratory at Teddington, and was definitely confirmed to be of terrestrial origin.

Meanwhile Pierre had shown Hans something that he longed

to see. On two of the bowls, as the patina came away, square incised panels had appeared; and in the panels an inscription in very early writing. They told him that the vessels were dedicated "to the House of Abu". Abu was a Lord of Vegetation, a title belonging also to Tammuz and Ninurta, the Lord of Plants and Slayer of Monsters.

Hans was certain now that the great copper hoard comprised the vessels used at ritual banquets, and quite definitely belonged to the little Temple; for after each New Year's Day Festival, when ceremonies took place to ensure the fertility of the crops for the coming year, there was always a ritual feast. Now he felt sure that the Temple must have been dedicated to the worship of Abu, Lord of Plants. The Herakles seal found there linked it with a fertility god who slew monsters, the jewellery found in the Palace—with its repeated motif of the lion-headed eagle—suggested a great ornament worn by a priest in the service of Ninurta. It seemed very likely, therefore, that the south-western part of the Palace had housed the officials of the Temple. Those ritual vessels must have been greatly prized, to have been collected together, packed down most carefully into a huge vessel and hidden right inside the thickness of a wall; a wall which had been very carefully plastered over afterwards, as though to make concealment doubly sure.

The reason, Hans thought, was not far to seek. Just at that point of time in the settled life of Eshnunna, terrible rumours must have been reaching the city of a great army of barbarian nomads, banded together under a mighty chieftain with an outlandish name, moving inexorably down the river valley from the north; rumours of city after city in the plain of Shinar falling beneath the onrush of Sargon. Fear was only too well founded; one could picture the sentries on the walls, and at the gates, staring out, day after day, over the green and peaceful plain which spread below them away to the far river; watching for the dreaded cloud of dust on the horizon, for the glint of sunlight on massed bows and spearpoints.

And while the sentries kept watch, behind them in the city the feverish preparation for a siege began, a siege which the people of Eshnunna must have known they could not long withstand—while the Temple officials swiftly stripped the holy place of its treasures, and carried them away to their own residence to seal them up inside a wall; in the desperate—and vain—hope that they would survive these dangerous times and live to see the day when the polished dishes would again be set out to grace their holy banquet. If that were too high a hope, then at least these vessels should never be touched by violent hands. They can never have seen them again. Yet they had saved them—as they must have prayed—from desecration; for from that moment of careful concealment no one had touched them until we ourselves had gently eased them out of the wall, marvelling at their numbers and at their workmanship.

·   ·   ·   ·   ·   ·

It was now nearly the end of February, and although, happily, we ourselves were not expecting the arrival of a marauding army, we could see almost daily now a haze or a column of dust southwards on the horizon, and often nearer.

"We have not had anything like enough rain this winter," Hans said, watching it uneasily. The sun blazed down every day; but often now a spiteful wind blew for a few hours, and then the gritty surface of the dry desert went scuffing up into the air, and streamed along on the wind, blinding and choking. One good downpour, every now and then, soaking the ground several inches deep, would have been enough to hold the dust and the sand, even if the wind blew hard for a while. But the rain never came; and the wind strengthened, and little whirl-winds ran about the land, hissing and whispering like malicious sprites, while yellow rivulets smoked and streamed across the grey, parched ground.

A letter came from Cairo. It was from James Henry Breasted, saying that he had completed his visit to Egypt and had decided to charter a plane and fly on to Iraq for a few days to see the dig before sailing for the States; and a few days later he arrived. The news spread quickly among the workmen that the Father of all the Digs had come.

The Father of all the Digs, for all his seventy-odd years, spent three days alertly absorbing every detail of our work, whether he was moving from point to point on the dig, or studying the plans in the drawing-office, or handling the finds, now lying, rank on rank, along the shelves of the antiquity room—taking in with a swift and practised eye everything that he was shown. Beneath the great brow and the fine sweep of silver hair, dark eyes looked out penetratingly, rather formidably; yet some-times twinkling and genial. For he had, in common with many rugged pioneers and great scholars, a happy lighter side; and on his last evening with us he sat reminiscing in a quiet, humor-ous voice of early days in Egypt. It was good to sit round the glowing fire in the living-room and watch his fine old head, and think: 'This is Breasted, who has brought all this about through his own vision and will—this vast chain of excavations sweeping up from Egypt, through Palestine, through Syria, and Iraq down to Persia.' I am glad that I had that one glimpse of him.

I remember one story of his of the tourist season at Luxor when, as a young man, he was busy copying an inscription at the base of a temple wall. It was below ground level, and a deep trench had been dug so as to reveal the lowest lines of hiero-glyphs. The only way he could get at it was to hang head downwards over the edge of the trench until not much more than his boots were visible from above. He heard a donkey-borne group of tourists passing, led by an English guide; an English, dowager-like voice asked (and Professor Breasted produced a very fair imitation of the breed), "What *can* that man be doing?" He heard the guide explaining that it was an archaeologist copying inscriptions. Breasted remained invisible except for his waving boots. Then, after a very long pause, "What an *extraordinary* way to earn your living!"

The next morning, a blowy and dusty morning, he drove away to the aerodrome at Baghdad; an hour or so later we heard the drone of a plane; he had asked his pilot to fly back, so that he could have a last glimpse of ancient Eshnunna from the air, before he left for Cairo. The Father of all the Digs was up there now, a thing of wonder to the workmen, most of whom had never seen an aeroplane; slowly it circled the Tell, while he looked down through the haze at the great Palace, the little Abu Temple, the clustering private houses with their streets and lanes, at the great southern Palace and the Gimilsin Temple. Then at last the plane wheeled round and headed west for far away Cairo; swiftly the haze hid it—for a few moments longer the engines pulsed faintly—and he was gone. It was his last sight of the Middle East.

· · · · · ·

The rain began that night; and all the next morning it poured down. By the afternoon Gabriel said he would not be able to move the water-lorry at all now for days so that we must be very careful of the water we had.

"I don't think I get even the light car through to Baghdad by now," he said, peering through the streaming window. For a little while everyone rejoiced at the freshness in the air, and in the knowledge that the ground was being well and truly soaked, the dust laid. Only for a little while. In the evening I met Yettie coming out of the boy's room. Her great eyes looked very anxious.

"He's very feverish," she said quickly. "I thought all day he wasn't himself; then he began to cry when I was putting him to bed, and said he had a pain, so I took his temperature—it's nearly 104."

My heart gave a horrible lurch. The sound of the drumming rain changed in a second from a joyful message of refreshment to something very sinister. We were already cut off from Baghdad, Gabriel had said, and the longer it went on raining now, the longer it would be before a car could possibly get through either way. There were good doctors in Baghdad, but there might as well be none, for all the help they could give us now.

It rained all night. In the morning Jon was no better, and Yettie said she thought he might have dysentery. She wrote a letter to the English doctor at the Hospital, explaining all the symptoms, and asking urgently for advice; one of the guards was told to saddle Hillai, and get through to Baghdad and back in the day, without fail. It was the best part of a hundred miles, most of the way through flooded and bogged desert. . . .

We watched him set off through the downpour under the dark sky, huddled in his brown cloak, Hillai splashing through the mud towards the track, now hidden completely under water. It seemed a very frail thread leading towards the help we so badly needed, and yet it was strangely comforting to feel that some plan, however tenuous, was under way.

The unhappy day dragged on; everyone seemed to avoid each other by mutual consent, and disappeared into their various work-places. No digging was possible, of course. For myself I got through a great deal of work at first, until I had sat by Jon for a little, while Yettie rested—then I went back to the office and couldn't work at all, sick with fear.

By nightfall there was still no sign of the guard, and we realised miserably that unless he had already got near enough to

" . . . gazed back at us with vast, unseeing, nightmare eyes."

Above Dr. Breasted, Hans and Jake in the Private House area.
Below Air view of Khafaje, showing Temple Platform, oval containing wall and, beyond, the Expedition House, cultivation and Dyala River.

see the light on the tower, he probably could not find his way back, with neither moon nor stars to help him. After dinner Yettie begged Rachel and me to come and talk in their room. We all sat there whispering to each other about the way small children rallied very quickly from high temperatures and tummy upsets—and did our best to believe it all; while from the next room Jon's voice murmured unhappily on and on, and we tip-toed in and out to do what we could for him. At one moment Hans said, "It's stopped raining." We pulled back the curtains and looked out. It had indeed stopped raining, but a sheet of unbroken water spread away far from the house, just visible under the lowering clouds. The dreadful flat expanse of weeping sky had given way to black rolling clouds, very low, slowly moving northward; here and there a dim star shone for a moment, and then vanished.

It was getting very late when a gentle tap came at the outer door. Hans opened it, and there was Gabriel, round face pale and unshaven, eyes full of tears. He adored Jon.

"I been on the tower, watching," he said in a husky whisper. "I think I see Mahmoud."

We ran through the door and up the stairs which led to the flat roof of the living-room; and stared out over the transformed land towards the drowned track. The black clouds parted, and just for a moment the whole world shone silver, an ocean seamed with long black reefs and islands.

Gabriel pointed. "There," he said suddenly; "he's against the sky now."

At first we could see nothing. And then—yes—something like a small bead sliding along the skyline of one of the nearer islands—it was Mahmoud's head, and he was fairly near by now. The clouds rolled over the moon's face, and the whole world sank back into utter darkness. But after a minute or two we could hear a faint sound of splashing, and then the moon shone again. Very slowly, limping a good deal, head drooping, Hillai was wading along the track towards us, Mahmoud huddled over her neck.

We went down to the front steps without speaking, and waited until he slid, slow and stiff, to the ground. He saluted wearily, but smiled faintly as he dragged a pouch off his shoulder and handed it to Yettie. In it was a large bottle of medicine and some tablets and a letter. The Syce came splashing round the corner of the house to take Hillai to the stable, and promised us that she would have a very good rub down and the feed of her life. Gabriel was told to see that Mahmoud had a hot meal; and they went off together under the tower, Mahmoud staggering, Gabriel's arm round his neck.

"He says he'll get out here as soon as he can," Yettie said, devouring the letter. "We'd better give the boy a little of the medicine now." Her face was very drawn, and Hans took her by the elbow; and we slipped away, as they went through into Jon's room.

The next day he was a little better, and a hot sun shone down on the steaming world; and much of the water had soaked away into the receiving ground. On the following day Gabriel said he thought he might get a car through to Baghdad, and set out very early, skidding and splashing. He arrived back in triumph with the doctor at about tea-time, who said he had never travelled so many miles sideways in his life before. He stayed the night, and said that Jon had indeed had a touch of dysentery, but was mending well. "As soon as he is fit to travel, get him out of here," he said as he left, "before the real dust-storms begin, or before there's any more rain, if possible. There hasn't been anything like enough rain this winter."

"I know," said Hans. "This is the first heavy rain out here—and already the ground is almost dry again in places."

Not many days later—only a few weeks before the normal

end of the season—Yettie and Jon set out together to drive with Gabriel to the airport, where they would begin the long flight to London.

Gabriel stowed the suitcases, and fussed round with rugs, crying hard all the time because Jon had been so ill, and because now he was all right, and because they were both going, and because Hans was left behind, and because—well, it was lovely having a good cry, anyway.

Jon sat quietly on Yettie's knee, not quite his jolly self, but wonderfully recovered and smiling, with his beret again on the back of his head, and his smart grown-up travelling coat on.

The car moved off, and we all stood waving on the steps until it disappeared behind the nearest hillock. We watched for a few minutes longer, until the car reappeared on higher ground much further off; a small black box balanced for a moment on the skyline. Then it dipped out of sight for good. It was a bad moment; a hateful moment for Hans.

Then Rigmor said, "See the heroine of the story." We turned to where she was looking. Through the open stable door stuck a long, gaunt, rocking-horse head, with a peering eye and a self-satisfied grin.

The tension eased away in laughter. Hans said to Seton, "I'm coming up right away to the Abu Temple. But first will someone please find me some lumps of sugar?"

CHAPTER SEVEN

ONE EVENING GABRIEL brought in a telegram from Gordon—a typically cautious telegram. It seemed to be in code, for it contained nothing but a reference to a large illustrated volume of which there was a copy in the Library cupboard, followed by 'see page 152'. It was all very exciting. The book was fetched; and we stood round while Hans leafed swiftly through it until he came to page 152. Sensation. It bore a small picture of some very dull bronze pins. Either Gordon was being altogether too fiendishly clever for us, or else there was a mistake. Hans sent off a telegram the next day which said: 'page 152 be damned what do you mean'; while the rest of us amused ourselves by being very funny about Gordon's spectacular find. Eventually a second telegram reached us: 'sorry telegraph office must have boobed try page 251'.

We tried page 251—and stopped being funny. It was a full-page illustration this time; and showed a magnificent winged bull carved in deep relief, which had been found some years earlier at Khorsabad, in Sargon II's Palace, one of a pair, each sixteen feet high and weighing about forty tons, that flanked the entrance to his Throne Room. It was obvious that Gordon must have discovered a new gateway in the Palace embellished with the same tremendous sculptured beasts. This was indeed a spectacular find, and he had wisely kept it as quiet as he could for the moment. A few days later a batch of photographs came, showing the early stages of the discovery. The top of the great human head of the bull, turbaned, with curled ringlets and beard, had been only a few feet below the modern ground level. So far, Gordon had only removed the concealing earth a few feet down below that—so that the head of the monster alone emerged truncated out of the earth, smiling benevolently, as if pleased to be released even thus far from his long captivity underground. He looked very odd and jolly; and I noticed in some of the photographs that there was real grass growing along the ground level, and—could it be true?—flowers in the grass. Khorsabad was not much more than 200 miles to the north of us—and soon we would be there.

But it was still three weeks before we were to leave Tell Asmar, and I forgot about flowers the next morning as I crossed the courtyard at breakfast time. The wind had been blowing hard in the night, and the little tree outside my courtyard window had thrashed and rustled ceaselessly, disturbingly. The sky above was cloudless, the sun blazing; but across the courtyard, just above the rooms that formed its southern side, there hung a long yellow fog, the like of which I'd never seen. Before going into the dining-room I went through to the front of the house, curious to see the look of things outside—and stared dismayed. The whole land was blotted out by a yellow curtain; even as I watched I could see that the upper limit of the haze to the south was rising every moment higher into the blue sky, reaching out thin groping fingers towards the sun.

Full of misgiving I went into the dining-room, which had no outer windows, and felt at once the gloomy tension among the others. As we breakfasted, a shadow passed over the room; and looking through the windows to the courtyard, we could see that the clear light had gone dim, and that the rooms opposite now stood in the nightmarish light of an eclipse.

"These storms nearly always bring rain-clouds eventually," Rachel remarked consolingly, and went off to the antiquity room. I went to the office, and after watching the southern sky for a few moments as it steadily darkened from yellow to a murky amber, put on the light and turned my back on the depressing sight. It was difficult to work. There was a sustained thrumming din, as the mounting wind buffeted angrily at every corner and surface that stood in its gigantic path, and sometimes hooted derisively as it found the narrow passageway outside the office door, and went hurtling through into the further courtyard. As it passed it flung the driven sand against door and windows with increasing force, so that it streamed in under the door, and little by little seeped even through the metal frames of the tightly closed windows; and gradually the room filled and darkened. Even when I brushed the dust off the lamp-bulb on the desk, the gleam hardly penetrated the choking haze. I looked over my shoulder. The sky was a hideous dark brown now, and I could scarcely make out the rooms across the courtyard.

I began to feel frightened; and thought I would take some work and go round to the antiquity room, telling myself that it would be a little more sheltered there—it had a double door, for one thing; though I knew, really, that what I wanted was company. The moment I turned the handle, the door burst open against me, and a great roaring cloud of acrid dust streamed all over me and into the room. I managed to get out and close the door, and then was blown round into the next courtyard. It was a good deal quieter in the antiquity room, but very dark. Rachel was there working, looking flushed and uncomfortable. After a while I began to wonder if it was nerves, or whether it really was getting difficult to take a proper breath.

"I don't think we've had such a bad one before," Rachel said slowly. "Sometimes they give me a bit of a temperature. We might try tying handkerchiefs over our mouths." We did this, and sat side by side for a little, looking up from time to time as we worked, at the window. By mid-morning there was no sky, no house, no ground—total darkness, howling, solid, menacing, pressed against the window. I thought of the house as we sometimes saw it from miles away when we were riding, a tiny brown toy dwarfed against the tremendous clouds. And now, that speck in the desert was lost in a raging blackness that weighed down upon it from who knows how many miles above; pressing down into our fragile insect lungs at every shallow breath.

We gave up working. After a while the outer door crashed open and slammed shut, and Hans came through the inner door. He had a damp scarf wound over his nose and mouth, which he now slipped under his chin.

"This is vile," he said huskily, coughing a little. "It's no good trying to work. I've told the cook to get us some kind of meal right away, and put it in the store-room—it's the most sheltered place—and after that we had all better go to ground in our rooms. Next year we must either stop digging earlier, or bring out gas-masks. I do not like this at all."

We followed him out, tying our handkerchiefs over most of our faces, and struggled round to the back door of the kitchen. The store-room opened out of it. The old cook and the Kurdish houseboy, Abdullah, had blocked the kitchen window with damp cloths, and had somehow got a table and chairs into the little store-room. One by one the others came in, looking like wilted gunmen on the run, eyes watering above dust-grimed scarves. Nobody talked much; nor could we eat much. But it was heartening to be together, wheezing at each other in the gloom, wedged between shelves full of tins of fruit and jam and sausages and carrots, bottles of salad cream and tomato-juice and pickles; our feet entangled with huge woven baskets full of eggs. Hans found several bottles of wine left over from Christmas on a shelf behind him, and commanded us to finish the lot, saying that it seemed a good moment. The black storm raged outside, and we sat there washing down the dust, and postponing the horrid journey through the open, back to our rooms.

When at last the party broke up, I rocked into my room, one part suffocated and three parts tiddly; feet crunching in the sand which had blown in under the door during the morning. I crept under the top covers on the bed and pulled them over my head, and tried not to panic. I had a pain in my chest, and my heart was racing. There was just one consolation; for a moment I had a small bright vision of Jon, playing somewhere in the clean, clear air on Hampstead Heath. Then, mercifully, I slid into a feverish, alcoholic stupor, and remained only vaguely conscious for the rest of the day.

There was someone tapping on my door—or was it the window? I roused up slowly, switched on the lamp, and croaked: "Come in." Nothing happened; but the tapping went on, quicker and louder. I pushed up my sleeve and saw that it was after ten o'clock. Odd. Then I looked round at the outer window that faced the desert. There were dark wet streaks chasing each other down the glass.

In a moment I was at the door and had flung it wide; and in sheer exhilaration skipped across the dry covered way into the open courtyard. It was pouring hard—but it was pouring mud. The rain had only just begun, and as it fell through the heavy pall was carrying down the sand with it. I retreated to my doorway, splashed with mud, and watched, breathing in the swiftly clearing air. Shapeless amber blotches began to loom through the haze and the rain; they were the lighted windows across the courtyard, the only evidence as yet of the hidden rooms there. Then, quite suddenly, as though one had successfully focused a blurred scene through field-glasses, the whole courtyard swam into view, sharp and solid, the windows once again brilliant rectangles, the supports of the covered way silhouetted black and trim against them. Doors began to open and more lights

Morning after a sandstorm.

Arbil—a modern town built on countless ancient towns.

Workman and boy—northerners of the Yezidi sect.

shone out, as the others emerged too to draw in the first blessed mouthfuls of clean air.

The dust was laid. But it went on pouring. I opened both windows to clear the room; and then got to bed, heedless of the chaos all round me, heedless of a stiff, dry skin and stinging throat; all I knew was that the horror was over, and that the sound of the rain was the loveliest music I had ever heard.

We became an excavation in our own right the following day, as the workmen dug us out with their hoes, and the basket-boys trotted away with tons of wet sand. A huge dune about the height of the rooms had formed along the outer south wall where the sand had beaten against it and then fallen back on itself—and the courtyards were heaped with drifted sand. Gradually the workmen found our floor-level for us, just as if we were ancient Sumerians. All the rooms had to be entirely cleared of furniture; every drawer taken out and shaken. Abdullah turned out all my clothes on to a sheet on the floor, indicating modestly as he pushed the chest of drawers out into the courtyard that the task of shaking them out was on me.

It took two days for the house to regain its trim clean order-liness; and then the workmen went back to their warren, for it was still raining. How they had survived that storm, huddled in their burrows, was difficult to understand. But apart from many of them presenting themselves at the medicine cupboard with sore eyes and coughs, none seemed much the worse.

When the rain stopped, Seton and Jake and Hal began to repair the damage on the dig, for a lot of clearance had to be done all over again. Meanwhile the desert lay tranquil under a soft spring sky, the ground dark and damp, with pools standing in all the hollows. The pools remained, day after day, only very gradually shrinking. It meant that the first rain, although it had sunk away so quickly that the surface had dried all too soon, must all the same have kept the hidden ground moist, which was now holding the new downpour on the surface.

When the house area on the dig had been cleaned up, Hans decided to stop digging there for this year, so that Hal would have time to catch up with his surveying; and Jake retired happily to the house to concentrate on the tablets and seal impressions which had been found during the season.

Seton was now far down in an earlier building of the Abu Temple, which Hans placed in the middle part of the Early Dynastic period, judging from the style of the cylinder seals found in it. The Temple was long and narrow, with a fine altar almost filling the western wall. Before the altar was a row of low mud-brick pedestals, which were tables to hold offerings, and there were small raised platforms against the southern wall.

"They may be for statues," Hans said. "It was a custom for worshippers to place their own representations in a Temple, as though to keep themselves continuously in the presence of the God. But at this level there hasn't been a sign of a sculptured fragment."

He asked Seton if he was ready for the final photography—he did not mean to go any deeper there either this season.

"Almost," Seton answered. "We've just got the ground level by the altar. They can start brushing now."

He told the workmen to begin cleaning the whole floor, and one of them took a big brush and began in the narrow right-hand niche between the altar and the northern wall. Seton watched him for a moment; and then stooped to pick something out of the fine dust which had been swept out of the corner. It was a chip of whitish stone, triangular in shape, smooth except for the base. He studied it for a moment. Anyone but a good field archaeologist would probably then have tossed the tiny thing away without another thought—but Seton happened to be a very good field archaeologist. He put it carefully into a matchbox, and the matchbox into his pocket. Rigmor arrived and spent the rest of the afternoon taking photographs of the cleaned up small Temple.

The next morning as I was typing in the office, I heard swift feet pattering past the door, and then saw a boy from the dig, Little Hussein, trot across the courtyard to the door of Hans' study. A moment later, Hans emerged and came quickly to the office.

"Give this boy all the things for getting out fragile stuff, will you?—and then come up yourself. Seton has some statues!"

He vanished; and I took Little Hussein round to the antiquity room and loaded him up with a large box full of knives and brushes and cotton-wool and small boxes. He trotted off. Rachel looked up inquiringly.

"Statues in the Temple," I said.

"Oh, wonderful!" she cried, throwing down her pencil. "I'll follow you up." I rushed off.

Seton and Hans were alone in the Abu Temple when I reached it. They were crouching in front of the niche beside the altar, and a fresh pile of rubble lay all round them on the clean floor. The niche was so narrow that they completely blocked it. I moved round them and climbed on to the lower part of the altar and peered over their heads.

"Look at this," Hans said. "Seton found that the floor was loose here."

Down in the floor of the niche was a long, oblong cavity— and in it I could see a gleaming, tightly packed mass of white and cream and grey and yellow stone statues; here a strange eye stared up, there a hand, long fingers curled round a cup, seemed to tremble with life as Seton gently brushed it with his fingers.

"Astounding," Hans said softly. "Let us begin to get them out."

He moved back and let Seton get at the hole freely. One by one he worked the statues loose, and handed them back to

Hans, and he and I laid them out on cotton wool on the hard ground. Most were over a foot in length. Many of them were broken, though all the pieces were in place; Hans said it looked as if they had been complete when buried, but that the weight of the numerous rebuildings of the Temple above must have cracked and crushed them. More statues came up, men and women, the men in fringed and tasselled kilts, the women with long cloaks thrown over one shoulder, leaving the other bare. All had their hands clasped before them, some holding cups. "They are worshippers, of course," Hans said.

Seton picked up some fragments and slid them into a box behind him.

"There are two more," he said. "But they are much bigger— I think I shall have to cut back the hole a good deal."

Rachel came through the Temple doorway, and stopped suddenly, transfixed at the sight on the ground. A long row of twelve stone figures, large-eyed, hands clasped, gazed up at her in mute prayer.

"Look at this, Rachel," Hans said.

Rachel looked, and gave a sudden cry, startled, marvelling, thrilled. Well she might, for gazing up at us out of the shadows were two pairs of appalling eyes—huge black eyes with gleaming white eyeballs. They were set in the faces of a bearded man and a woman, each holding a cup. Rachel, speechless with excitement, stood back and Seton began the task of extracting them. Gradually he freed them from the surrounding earth; then at last put down knife and brush and got both his arms down into the cavity. The statues were cracked in places, but almost complete; and at last they were brought up and set beside the others. They were indeed much larger and heavier, the male figure over two feet in height. Like the rest, they stood on heavy stone pedestals.

For a moment no one said anything. We gazed at them; and

they gazed back at us with vast, unseeing, nightmare eyes. When I could drag my own away, I saw that the woman's pedestal had a small niche cut in it by her left leg; and in this niche her child had once stood—the small feet were still there.

"She must be the Mother Goddess with her son," said Hans. His face was rather white under his sunburn. I think he was becoming exhausted under the pressure of his elation, and under the terrific new stimulus which must have kept his thoughts racing all through this incredible event.

The man had a mass of jet-black hair and a long, rippling beard; the hair had been coloured with bitumen. The white eyeballs had been cut from shell; and the huge irises, of black stone, had been fixed into circles cut out of the shell.

"He is quite astounding," Hans murmured, shaking his head a little. "A pity he just lacks the end of his nose; for otherwise he is complete."

Seton bent down and examined the broken tip—then suddenly: "I *wonder* . . ." and whipped out a matchbox—and picked out of it a chip of whitish stone, triangular in shape, smooth except for the base. . . . We watched breathlessly while he brought it towards the fantastic upturned face, and neatly set the fragment in place. It fitted exactly.

After a moment, Hans said, "I believe there is some carving on his pedestal." The dust was still clinging to all the figures; and he swiftly but carefully brushed the front of the great statue's deep pedestal. As the dust streamed down, a fine panel of incised relief work was revealed. Two gazelles crouched peacefully, back to back, like heraldic figures, while leafy branches curled along behind them; and between them hovered with outstretched wings the lion-headed eagle, Imdugud.

"Shepherd of the flocks, Lord of Vegetation," Hans said, very quietly. "This is the God of the Temple—Abu himself."

. . . . . .

It was an unique find; not only because of the number of statues found together in one hoard, but also because of the early date of the sculpture. Nothing to equal it had ever been found before in excavations in Mesopotamia—or has been since. Very little free carving in the round had been done before this period, and then it consisted mainly of small figurines. But here, without any apparent background of slow sculptural development, appeared these strange angular figures, carved with great mastery, balanced between the representation of human figures and sheer abstract form. They looked as if the ancient sculptors, setting out to portray men and women at prayer in a Temple, had been far more preoccupied with the idea of worship itself than with the forms of the frail humans who brought this worship to the God: or rather, the form was there, but very much simplified and made subordinate to a more than human idea.

The bodies were sharp-edged, the facial features rudimentary, and the legs colossally thick, in order to support the considerable weight of stone above—and yet, the quiet balanced pose, the slightly raised humble shoulders, the clasped hands, the upturned awe-inspired faces expressed with absolute competence the essential feeling of worship. They were the vigorous work of men, at the beginning of a settled, civilised period, not long after 3000 B.C., on fire with an urge quite new to the ancient world—to translate for the first time deep feeling into terms of carving in the round; an urge that has never since died down among craftsmen working in wood and stone.

Unlike the hoard of copper vessels and knives belonging to a later building of the Abu Temple, the statues had not been buried to save them in troubled times, Hans thought. There was no evidence of some violent change, which signs of fire or of a new building technique just above it would have suggested. The little Temple had been rebuilt peacefully over them. It looked as if it was the custom, when the Temple was rebuilt, for the statues of worshippers and Gods to be renewed also; so that the present ones had been carefully gathered up and laid to rest in dedicated ground close to the altar. Fragments of other statues had been found in the later, higher levels, and these might indeed be all that was left of statues still in use at the time of the Akkadian conquest. The statues of the hoard certainly hadn't been buried because they were worn out. All the angles were sharp, the surfaces unblurred by time; the colour of hair and beards was fresh and dark; and almost every crack and breakage had been caused, as I have said, by the weight of the superimposed rebuilding on the tightly packed figures. The pressure must have been tremendous, for across the kilt of one worshipper, front and back, were the clear impressions of the kilt fringes of the two statues above and below him, pressed right into the yellow limestone from which he was carved.

Rigmor, who had thought that with the final photography of the Abu Temple out on the dig, and of the copper hoard indoors, her season's work was as good as completed, began all over again. As each statue was registered, cleaned and repaired, she set to work on it; with Hans eagerly demanding front views, back views, profiles; close-ups of heads, and hands, and feet, and pedestals.

"We must have every photograph possible done here," he said. "The God and Goddess will certainly go to Baghdad at the Division, and probably most of the others; so we *must* get our publication plates right away—no one will ever produce better ones than you, Rigmor."

Rigmor gave a desperate laugh, and battled on against time—and, needless to say, achieved a magnificent set of photographs by the end of the season.

The day of the Division came. The new Director of

Antiquities, who had dug at Erech for many years, came out to make the selection for the Baghdad Museum; a handsome, white-haired, blue-eyed German, with a wonderful tenor voice. He was genial, and interpreted the Antiquity Law leniently from our point of view. This law had been drawn up by Gertrude Bell eight years earlier, when she had become the first Director of Antiquities in Iraq. It stated that anything unique found by the Excavator should be retained for the collections of the country in the Museum at Baghdad; and that after that, the remaining finds should be divided fairly between the Department of Antiquities and the Excavator. As Hans expected, the God and Goddess were taken for the Museum, where they stand to this day. But the Director released several of the other statues for Chicago, each of which, although alike in some respects, were unique in one way or another, and could quite lawfully have been assigned to Baghdad.

Hans was pleased with the result of the Division; and late in the evening the Director, blue eyes twinkling, Auf Wiedersehned himself off to Baghdad. We didn't know then that he was one of Hitler's bluest-eyed boys, busily using his unique position in Baghdad as a channel for ideas—and more than ideas—to come filtering through from Berlin. While King Feisal I still lived, shrewd and sensitive, with a strong hand on affairs, all this ran very deep underground. But Feisal died the following year, and those men of Iraq who had supported him loyally, suddenly found themselves faced with an ugly situation, with rascally elements in Government and Army seeking power, backed by funds and arms which had reached the country through the agency of the bland old archaeologist pottering round his glass cases in the Museum, humming Lieder.

But this was still in the future; here I was in the courtyard outside the antiquity room, packing down the finds which had

144

Varieties of
winged life at
Khorsabad.

The Mukhtar of Jerwan
seated on blocks inscribed with fragments of the exploits of Sennacherib.

Seton and Jake standing on the aqueduct.
The village of Jerwan is beyond.

been left to us into cases, while Gabriel stencilled the address of the Oriental Institute, and 'In Bond to Chicago' in huge black letters on the lids. There was an end-of-term feeling; especially after the final payday, when the last black specks had vanished towards the north to settle again beside their mud huts and onion patches, under the shade of the palm-groves, for the long, hot summer; while utter silence drifted down over the gashed and empty Tell.

Rachel and I had been packing antiquities all day long, looking at many of them for the last time, unless some unexpected turn of the wheel should take us one day to Chicago. It was a long business, whether we were filling small boxes with alternate layers of cotton wool and the smaller objects, or whether we were working out the problem of the safest method of packing the large pots and statues and copper.

None of our problems compared with one which had occupied Pierre a few years earlier, at the end of a season; for it was he who had packed and transported the winged bull—of page 251—from Khorsabad to the bank of the Tigris, a matter of fifteen miles, en route for Chicago. The huge relief, with its stone background, weighed forty tons, and the only available lorry about fifteen. He had the whole sculpture sawn into several pieces; even then the largest piece weighed nineteen tons. One by one they made the journey on the lorry along a narrow crazy mud track running alongside the Khosr river to the sloping bank of the Tigris, where a small cargo-steamer lay waiting to carry the fragments down to a large ship at Basra. Hawsers were fixed to the great nineteen-ton crate, and the winch set in motion. The hawsers tautened and strained—and nothing else happened. It seemed as if the bull were loth to leave his fatherland; loth to try the hazards of a new element. The winch groaned into action once more with all available power, and the tug-of-war began again. And the bull nearly won—for while it remained motionless on the bank, the small steamer was suddenly seen to be doing its best to climb sideways up the bank. In the end, the reluctant and dismembered monster was somehow heaved on board; and to-day adorns the end of a great Museum hall in Chicago. Insults and injuries forgotten, he stands serene, all in one piece, not a scar showing, purring over the heads of all the marvelling visitors. . . .

After a late tea Rachel and I shook the shavings out of our hair and went for a walk southwards, for we had seen the tops of a few black tents not far away. Across the track we went, and on between the hillocks, still moist and quiet; and as the level light of the sun, now low in the west, struck the dunes, we saw a wonderful thing—they shone pale green. A thin growth of tender grass spread like a haze over all the ground; and as we rounded a bastion of sand, and came to a long, shallow depression where a great pool had stood for many days, we found the grass in the dip thick and brilliant, gold-tipped in the sunshine. The water had almost vanished now, but a few little shining pools, reflecting the springtime sky, still lay here and there, grass blades spearing up through them. But the pools were outshone by another blue, intense yet tender, that ringed them; for there were hundreds of little blue irises flowering in the grass. They came up every year for a very brief time, to vanish with the grass almost overnight, as the merciless sun sucked the last meagre drops of moisture from the frail roots. If only this land could be irrigated again, we thought, how wonderful it might be. Small birds were wheeling above the flowers. We walked on through the little paradise of blue and green and gold, until we came to the small encampment. Some nomad shepherds had settled by another pool; the tents were rough shelters made of black goatskin, the sides rolled up in this gentle weather; a woman was cooking over a fire of dry scrub.

146

The shepherds rested near the tents, while small black goats were dotted all over the dunes, eagerly nibbling at the tender grass. A little boy carrying a new-born kid came toddling up, laughing and chattering, and tried to give it to us. We fondled the long silky black ears, and then turned homeward, while the baby wandered off again to the tents.

It was difficult to remember on this quiet glowing evening that this land had been lashed up into the raging fury that we had known such a little while ago. I'd seen the desert now in many of its moods. Cold and dead, like the moon; a silver ocean, studded with uninhabited islands; a black, suffocating hell; and now—serene and beautiful, idyllic. We picked some irises, and the sun went down. As we neared the house a full moon rose above the snow-peaks of the distant mountains, a moon already brilliant even while the sunset glow still lingered. I noticed an odd thing that had never happened to me before— I had two shadows, spread out on either side along the now colourless ground; one from the sunset glow; and one, paler, from the rising moon. Ahead of us to the north a great jewel of a star had just risen and lay on the horizon, with another hanging not far above it. They were, I knew, the pointers of the Great Bear. I'd often watched him swinging up from his underground lair night after night—for down in this latitude he wasn't a circumpolar bear any more, as in England, where he swings eternally free of the northern horizon. It was easy to see why the stars had first been studied as a science in this part of the world, where they blaze at eye-level all around as soon as darkness falls.

There was no time to think about astronomy or anything else much for the next few days. Hans and Seton and the Jakes left for the north; they were planning to investigate an idea of Jake's that he had been turning over in his mind since the last visit to Khorsabad. Rachel and Hal and I would do the final closing down and follow in three days' time; and the Khafaje people soon after that. I spent those days packing immense parcels—all the precious negatives and prints and registration pages and drawings and notebooks and correspondence—wondering if I would ever find all this vital information safe at the other end of the long journey to the little office in Sicilian Avenue. Then there were inventories to check, and precious gramophone records to store away as carefully as possible; we put them in the darkroom, which was the coolest place, to save them from warping, even from melting (which had once happened) in the intense heat of the summer, which might rise to 130 degrees at times.

Then early one morning Gabriel drove us away to Baghdad, and the white figures of tall Abdullah and the little old cook and the dark cloaked guards standing below the tower quickly dwindled against the sun-soaked walls of the silent house. We swung round the shoulder of a sand dune, and Tell Asmar vanished. I felt an odd sensation, which I certainly hadn't expected, and would not have thought possible a few months ago—a wrenching feeling, almost like homesickness. Something in the bleak land with its vast skies, its empty quiet, had already sunk into me, telling me that I should never know—in spite of its occasional sulks and tantrums—such silence, such space, such peace, anywhere else in the world. Just now I was tired from the long season's work, tired from the real strain of that last sandstorm, eager for the move to the north; yet I knew—as we lurched along the track, up and over the banks of the old canals—that already I was secretly glad that in the autumn, if Allah willed, I would come back to the desert.

·　·　·　·　·　·

At lunch-time I emerged from the only hairdresser in New Street, feeling like a curled Assyrian bull. It was very nice to have a glossy head of hair again, although when I met the others for lunch they reeled under the impact of all the scented sprays with which the little Turkish hairdresser had seen fit to finish off his handiwork. He had a violent cast in one eye, which may have accounted for the rather meandering effect of my new parting. I asked Hal doubtfully if it seemed straight to him, and after inspecting it gravely he said it reminded him a little of an alley-way that had baffled him between some houses in Early Dynastic II. After lunch we found our way to the Bazaar. The cobbled lanes twisted this way and that, the sunlight filtering down into the narrow canyons between the flapping cloths and matting which passed for roofing. Stray beams of dusty sunlight fell on the jostling crowds, and on the patient, loaded backs of the small donkeys titupping by; and struck a little way back into the mysterious caverns on either side, where the merchants stored and sold their goods. Dim figures lolled in the shadows at the back of these booths, or squatted by their huge scales; others, at the front of the caverns, sunlit, lazily watched the passing crowds, or called their wares. There were booths piled high with fabrics, often tawdry, but some rich and fine; booths with all kinds of fruits and sweets, with great rings of fly-blown pastry stacked on long rods, as if someone had just won a fantastic game of Hoopla. Some had curtains of dangling shoes swaying on strings, red and blue and green shoes, tasselled and curled up at the toes, framing the tops and sides of the caves; or sprouting from poles· like Christmas trees.

We drifted on with the crowd, until we came to the corner of the Bazaar where the coppersmiths worked. The din to our unpractised ears was shattering, as little men beat on trays and bowls and coffee-pots and kettles, the sunlight pricking and flashing on the vibrating metal through the warm gloom. The little hammers clicked and tapped and rang and banged, and the crowds jostled by, laughing and quarrelling and yelling. Surely so many people couldn't be true. . . .

Then we were back in New Street. The afternoon was slipping away; the narrow street, saturated all through with an overwhelming smell compounded of petrol fumes, cooking oils, dust, spices, decaying vegetation and river mud, was already half in shadow. But above the smells and the bustle—the little open carriages clattering along, the honking cars, the crowds, the occasional maimed and terrible beggar—a great golden dome rose into the upper air, full in the sunshine from across the river. A flock of iridescent pigeons, purple and blue and green, rested on its gleaming shoulder, as though it were stuck all over with vast opals.

We turned down an alley and in at a side door, the shop of the Kashi brothers; one of the little men, melancholy and filmy-eyed with over-much hashish, welcomed us, and sent a boy to bring cups of coffee; we sat in the half-light, in blessed quiet, under a lamp glowing in the shadows like a great ruby, while he wandered into the depths of his treasure cave, and brought out fine rugs, and wonderful Persian brocades, and shawls, and silken scarves, shot with green and gold, rose and lilac, blue and silver.

"A caravan from Persia just arrived," he murmured, and went back to fetch some more.

So the caravans still came jingling through the mountain passes, through the foothills, down into the level plain, bringing with them the treasures of the East. Kashi's clouded eyes seemed to be watching the camels and the donkeys and the drivers, passing to and fro, to and fro, along the golden road to Samarkand.

Time fled. Then: "I think I *must* have this as well," said Rachel softly, lifting another shimmering beauty from the glowing heap of colour on the floor.

"And I must have this, too," I said. It was an exquisite golden square of brocade, showered with tiny turquoise birds and rainbow-hued flowers.

"And I *know* I must have this," said Hal, sensitive fingers smoothing a dark crimson, silken wrap. His tired eyes were sparkling.

At any time Kashi's wares would have been difficult to resist, but to us, newly come from the wasteland, thirsty for colour and soft richness, they were intoxicating. Little Kashi was in a position to buy a lot more hashish, to set him a-dreaming of beauty beyond this earth, by the time we left him; he stood at his door, faintly smiling, already withdrawing into his private world.

Gabriel had somehow found out where we were—and was waiting in the street with the car. He stowed our precious parcels, and said that we had better go to the station right away, for the train to the north left in an hour.

At the station across the river, he bought us second-class tickets and put us into a first-class carriage, with some garbled tale about "speshul conseshun for archaeologist peoples". Rachel was dubious, and the stationmaster even more so; he was a great friend of Gabriel's, needless to say; but we ought to be in a second-class carriage, he said. Gabriel slapped him, bellowed with laughter, and countered with the Arabic equivalent of: "O.K., so you turn them out."

The little man became angry, and stamped.

Gabriel took him by the collar, and began to throttle him.

"It is the University of Chicago!" he shouted, playing his favourite card, his bulging eyes close to his victim's face.

Rachel, not wishing to witness murder, leaned out of the window and begged to be allowed to get into a second-class carriage. Hal and I sat tight, giggling.

The train jerked into life.

Our last glimpse of Gabriel that season was of him standing with one arm round the stationmaster's neck, waving his hat and wreathed in smiles. The stationmaster, with his tie under one ear, was smiling and waving too.

CHAPTER EIGHT

It took us over twenty-four hours to reach Mosul. The Berlin–Baghdad railway, begun before the First World War and then of course abandoned, was still incomplete, with a gap of 100 miles or so on either side of Mosul. In the early hours of the morning we were decanted at the southern terminus, not much over 100 miles north of Baghdad, into a desolate plain, with outcrops of rock breaking the boulder-strewn ground— but the rocks and boulders were lapped by a sea of rippling grass, blowing in the fresh breeze of a grey dawn. As the light grew stronger I saw that the eastern mountains were much nearer now; for the rocky eastern frontier of Iraq leans north-westerly all the way from the Persian Gulf up to Asia Minor. The mountain streams flowing down from the heights spill ever further westward into the grateful plain, reaching towards the Tigris and bringing this northern land to green life as they wind on their way.

We travelled on by car, diverting a little to the north-east to see a walled town which is said to be the oldest continuously inhabited city known. This is Arbil; we could see it from afar in the plain as the morning sun struck it, built on a high, sharply sloping hill. The mound, grass covered, is formed of the rebuilt cities of thousands of years, just as Tell Asmar and all the other cities of the plain had slowly risen up from ground level. But, whereas their days had ended long ago, the mounds flattened and desolate, drifted over with sand and pebbles and potsherds, Arbil still flourishes as a living city, perching higher and ever higher as the citizens continue to pull down an old

house here, a disused workshop there, and run up new buildings over the roughly levelled foundations. We climbed up a
steep ramp, treading as we went over the buried houses of
ancient cities, to the gateway of the modern town; and
wandered through dark alley-ways to the Bazaar. It was as if
the House Area at Tell Asmar had come to life; for Hal's alley-
ways and courtyards had simply grown high walls again, the
little houses walls and roofs, and hummed with talk and
laughter, all the hubbub of crowded humanity. The shape of
the windows and the doorways facing on the little streets was
just the same as those which he and Jake had found in a city
more than 4000 years older. Arbil has probably kept very
much the same plan of streets and houses through all its long
history.

We came out of the dark, mazy hive at last to the town gate,
and stood dazzled at the top of the ramp, looking out over the
great sunlit plain to the south; it was very silent now, but for
the faint music of the wind moving over the leaning grass. No
ghostly hooves thundering by, nor clash of metal; no shouts of
Grecian triumph, nor thin cries of Persian despair. For down
there, beneath the walls of old Arbil, Darius made his final
stand against young Alexander, who, drunk with the dream of
limitless Empire, had spurned the Great King's offer of the
western lands as far as the Euphrates, and had come storming
on.

We reached Mosul after dark, exhausted after the rough
drive back to the river, to a point where a ferry took us across
to the western bank on which Mosul stands. The ferry had
stuck in mid-river on a sand-bank, and we waited nervously for
a long time as the sun set, while a very old Arab, alone with
his problem and a long pole, pottered about on and off the
sandbank, trying to refloat himself. Near us, four wild-looking
northerners, Kurds, black curls hanging to their shoulders,

knives in their coloured twisted belts, squatted on the bank and watched us intently, muttering, argumentative, as if they were not quite in agreement as to how soon after sundown you could reasonably expect to get away with murder. Maybe they were most innocent souls simply deeply curious about us and our business there, and indulging in a Kurdish variety of Twenty Questions on the subject; but there had been several incidents lately in these parts—one or two including murder—when benighted travellers had been held up by lawless characters, and this heightened our discomfort; so that the bumping of the crazy old ferry against the bank was a very welcome sound just as the last sunset glow was fading. On again northward as the night closed down, along the western shore of the Tigris now. We were on the same road that had been trodden by those weary prisoners-of-war taken after the fall of Kut, on their ghastly march hundreds of miles northward to Turkey. The road circled the base of a great hill soaring into the sky to our right—it was ancient Assur that was blotting out the stars; capital of mighty Assyria, bearing the name of its ancient tribal god. At its foot a few low huts clustered, a dim light showing here and there; it was odd, and pleasant, as we plunged past, on into the dark again, to think that our own Shergatis were in those huts, just back from their labours at Tell Asmar and Khafaje, chunnering away in the bosoms of their admiring families; travelled, wealthy men with five months' wages still intact, not to mention their travel allowances. . . .

It had been very comforting, a little later, to see the lights of Mosul twinkling not far ahead.

We stayed for the night at the Rest House, a railway hotel without a railway, high and dry between its two distant termini; I don't suppose anywhere else in the world one would have to drive 100 miles through difficult country to get from the railway station to the Station Hotel. I was so exhausted on arriving, that it never occurred to me to be even mildly surprised that two enormous turkeys were wandering about the passage outside my room, gently gobbling their greetings.

The next morning we drove out of Mosul, through its golden spinney of delicate minarets, through the narrow, sunny streets into the glittering air of the countryside again, towards the nearby bridge spanning the Tigris—for Khorsabad lies to the east of the river. We crossed the Tigris; ahead lay a long, low, grass-covered barrier. The sandy road wound through a breach in its green banks; and we went on northeast across peaceful agricultural country. Nothing to show that this quiet ploughland crossed only by the road and by a small sparkling river, had once teemed and rung with thronging crowds and chariots and soldiers—for those green banks we had passed between were the western walls of ancient Nineveh, and we were now crossing the site of the city itself. Here came Jonah, bravely preaching the word of the Lord after his backsliding. The ancient word for Nineveh has a definite connection with the ancient Semitic word for "fish", and there is a theory that the great whale into which he disappeared for three days was simply a translator's error for the huge teeming maze of the city which swallowed him up for a few days until he emerged as prophet and preacher.

A mile further on, still hand in hand with the little river, we passed through the eastern walls. The river was the Khosr, after which the modern village of Khorsabad is named; it was this river, much wider and stronger and deeper then, which had long ago breached the eastern wall of Nineveh, that gap through which we and it had just peacefully ambled; and, flooding much of the huge city, had weakened its final stand against its enemies.

The beauty of the land, now unfolding, began to make me feel light-headed. The country up here would seem beautiful at any time—but now, seeing it for the first time after the months in the southern wasteland, there seemed too much for eyes to tell brain; a convalescent brain that almost needed to have the meaning of colour and form explained to it anew. Perhaps it would have been altogether too much, but for that faint foretaste, that glimpse of transient beauty one evening near Tell Asmar.

We were rising a little now, drawing nearer all the while to high green hills still a few miles ahead. The ploughland on either side of the rough track held the rich red warmth of Devon, the thick grass was brilliant; great fields of yellow mustard rose against the soft spring sky, and snow-peaks lifted into the clear air beyond the hills. The ditches ran with sparkling water and everywhere the grassland was splashed and sprinkled with scarlet anemones and flaring wild tulips.

We plunged along the road. Sargon, the father of Sennacherib, had built it himself towards the end of the eighth century B.C., when he founded his new capital out here. We were very near the foothills now. To our left just beyond the river, a group of little thatched houses stood beneath tall trees. This was the village of Khorsabad. And close to the track on the other side, a great mound loomed up. This was the hill which Sargon had built, on the top of which he placed his Palace, astride the city wall. The track ran on, curling into the hills through a low pass. But now the driver slowed down, turned off the road, changed to his lowest gear, and charged up a short steep mud ramp which brought us to the great flat area at the top. We had come up to the gates of Sargon's Palace.

Here at this height he could keep watch on the mountains to east and north, on the plain to the west, and over his new walled city, which all lay to the south of the Palace. Here he came up from Nineveh with his young heir, Sennacherib, along the road which he had made, that same road which we had traversed. Here Sennacherib spent his boyhood, while the armies of his father swept over vast areas, and brought terror and desolation to all who stood in the path of mighty Assyria. Listen to Nahum the prophet: "He that dasheth in pieces is come up before thy face. The chariots rage in the streets, they jostle one against the other in the broad ways; the appearance of them is like torches, they run like the lightnings." And then he foretells the fall of Assyria, crying: "Where is the den of the lions, where the lion walked and the lion's whelp, and none made them afraid? Behold, I am against them, saith the Lord of hosts."

The area at the top of this great mound had been large enough to contain a Palace and three Temples—yet the whole construction had been built of small sun-dried bricks; a colossal undertaking. One thought again of another gaunt host of war-prisoners marching to enforced labour in a hostile land; for this was probably how so many workmen were available.

On the south-west corner of the platform a small grass-grown hillock rose up, the crumbled remains of a Temple tower, Sargon's ziggurat—and in the centre of the platform stood the Expedition House. It looked pleasantly ramshackle and small in contrast to the trim sweeping lines of the house at Tell Asmar. A long, mud-plastered brown wall faced west-ward towards Mosul; it was roughly thatched and was pierced in the centre by a great square opening, in and out of which casual hens and a turkey or two were strolling in the sunshine. Gordon came through the doorway suddenly, having just heard our car grinding up the slope; shy and smiling and welcoming. He told us that Hans and Seton and the Jakes had gone off into the hills beyond, but that Hans was expected back that evening. He led us through the doorway, and I saw that the house consisted of one big grassy courtyard, surrounded by small rooms. My own room was on the eastern side; it was like a tiny cottage, for the thatched, sunny doorway had white paving-stones at the sill, on either side of which great dark blue hyacinths and pale jonquils were scenting the warm air. I remained light-headed. The little room had a small window looking out eastward, and through it I could see, beyond the house, a terrace of grass about ten feet wide ending abruptly like the edge of a cliff, for part of the excavated Palace lay there. Beyond a wide gap the mound sloped gently down on this side to lush fields, to rise again quite near very steeply, up and up to the wonderful sky-line of the great green hills. Looking over to the left, I could just see the white road curling on through the grass towards a cleft in the hills, and in the distance, filling the background of the pass, the unbelievable snow-peaks which I knew I could never look upon for long enough.

The house was an old native one, built over a small part of Sargon's Palace; it was all that was left of a settlement up here made by the Khorsabad villagers. When further excavation of the Palace had made it imperative to get them to move some years before, the villagers would not budge, in spite of handsome offers of compensation in exchange for their uprooting. They were always healthy up here, they said; they were always taking a terrible fever down there across the road. It was a dilemma. Pierre went down to have a look at the abandoned village at the foot of the mound, and discovered a large stagnant pond humming with mosquitoes; he dug a channel from it to the river nearby, and away went the pond and the mosquitoes; and after a little further persuasion the villagers decamped, never to suffer fresh outbreaks of malaria again. The houses on the mound were now pulled down, all except one, and the excavations went on, right up to the walls of the Expedition House.

After lunch Gordon showed Hal and me round the top of the mound. We stood on the edge of the grass terrace behind the house and looked down into a very long paved room running north and south. At the southern end there were remains of steps leading up to a great stone throne which rose out of a tangle of flowers and grass.

"This is Sargon's Throne Room," Gordon said. "The entrance from the outer courtyard is over there." He pointed to the long side of the room opposite us, where a wide gap cut the deep wall. In the gap itself, a few fragments of white stone gleamed in the grass.

"It was there that they found the winged bulls, one of which is in Chicago," he went on. "They flanked that entrance leading from the courtyard into the Throne Room."

We went round the house to the western side of the mound again, and looked out over the vast plain. The track and the river went curving away together towards far-off Mosul; we could just make out the faint outlines of the eastern walls of Nineveh, but a river-mist hung over the Tigris beyond, shrouding the horizon. Far away to the south I could see a cone-shaped mound, lifting brown and solid out of the green plain.

"Nimrud," said Gordon. "It was the capital of Assyria after Assur and before Nineveh. Assur is in the same direction, but very much further on, beyond the river—too far to see." We told him that we had passed it late the night before.

All through this ancient echoing land one was conscious of the language of Genesis. Babylon—Erech—Akkad; Assur—Nineveh—and now—Nimrud; its name perhaps, like Assur, reflecting a dim memory of an ancient legendary god-hero: "And Cush begat Nimrud; he began to be a mighty one in the earth. He was a mighty hunter before the Lord: wherefore it is said, Even as Nimrud the mighty hunter before the Lord.

And the beginning of his kingdom was Babel, and Erech, and Accad, and Calneh, in the land of Shinar. Out of that land went forth Asshur, and builded Nineveh. . . ."

Quite near us down at ground level on the south side of the mound the plan of a great building cut down into the grass-land, swarming with workmen and basket-boys. I could see head-shawls of flaming orange and glowing crimson—great twisted belts of blue and green and purple—an occasional glint of white linen. It seemed as if the men of this sparkling paradise could not have enough of colour, but must swathe their dark faces and lithe figures in like brilliance.

"The new bulls are there," said Gordon. "Come down and have a look at them."

The paved floor of the building was about twenty feet below the modern ground level; we walked between high cliffs of red earth, crowned with grass and yellow daisies; then turned a corner and suddenly came upon the fantastic gateway, flanked with the two colossal monsters. They were breathtaking. Gordon had now cleared them both completely, down to the floor; his men had moved countless tons of earth since the moment when he had first encountered the top of one head a little way below ground level.

They shone white, and gazed serenely out with bland eyes far above our heads, great wings sweeping away over their proud backs. These tremendous monsters were the original "cherubs" of the Old Testament, combining two aspects which were wonderfully expressed in the contrast between their be-nign, smiling, bearded faces and their fiercely aggressive bodies. They were serene divinities protecting the King who had set them at his gates, but also fiercely on guard to subdue all evil that might approach him.

Gordon was almost as worried about them as he was pleased. He said that since the news of their discovery had got about he had had a stream of visitors coming out from Mosul to look at them, and in spite of the guards left at the site between seasons, he was uneasy when he thought of the vandal who likes to carve his initials on an antiquity, or even chip away a piece of it for a souvenir. He was coming to the conclusion—expensive in terms of the workmen's wages though it would be—that the best way out would be to re-bury them. This was what he did at the end of the season; but the cherubim suffered only a temporary eclipse this time, for today they stand proudly in Baghdad, very suitably flanking the entrance to the new Museum there.

As we climbed to the top of the mound again, a car shot up the ramp on the far side, and Hans jumped out; a very brown and cheerful Hans, carefree and open-at-the-neck, carrying his jacket over his arm.

"So you are here—goot!" he called to us. "This country— *mon Dieu!*—we have been far too long away from flowers— you should see them at Jerwan—but I must tell you about it— the others will stay there for a month, and will have equipment sent them tomorrow. Gordon, please may we have some tea? And out in the courtyard? I cannot be away from the grass."

We all moved through the gateway and soon were sitting in the sun, listening to him. He was extending the Expedition in order to follow up a clue which Jake had come across the year before, while Gordon continued to direct the work at Khorsabad. To use a naval metaphor, Hans wore his flag in Khorsabad as Admiral-strategist, while leaving Gordon to carry on as its unquestioned Captain, which he did with immense efficiency.

Sargon's city was in any case of secondary interest to Hans, even though he could admire the splendour of its conception; however wonderful the organisation which Sargon had built up, it was mainly aimed at carrying out vast schemes of conquest, accompanied by merciless cruelty. The cold, competent chiselling of the reliefs that tell the story of Sargon's prowess in war or in the hunt, left him equally as cold, both in their subject-matter and in their execution; their polished, conscientious technique spoke to him of decadence and death, of sculptors obeying a weary convention, late in time—and 700 B.C., odd though it sounds, seems very late in time to those who have been thinking in terms of 2000, 3000, even 4000 B.C. His happiness up here sprang entirely from the beauty that surrounded him; conversely, in the south, where the desert land weighed heavily on his spirits, the work itself completely engrossed him. For down at Tell Asmar he was near to the beginning of history, near its shadowy dawn, where he moved ever deeper into an uncharted territory, in the fitful light of each new discovery, a pioneer; where eager men, only lately emerged from a struggle for mere existence, were experimenting with untutored hands for the first time in stone and metal, creating things which reflected the trend of their thrusting minds. It was in this that Hans' deepest interest lay—in the interpretation, by means of material remains, of the thought of early man throughout the ancient world. Already, I knew, he was deeply preoccupied with a comparative study of Egyptian and Mesopotamian sculpture, and the difference of outlook which it demonstrated, in the new light shed by the hoard of statues from the Abu Temple.

Meanwhile here he was eating buns in the sunshine, and gaily telling us about Sennacherib. He had, I think, a softer spot for Sargon's son, who, although there wasn't much to choose between father and son when it came to their bloody exploits in the field, at least had a passion, which his father lacked, for planting things; and Hans himself was a great and knowledgeable gardener.

When Sennacherib succeeded in 705 B.C., he abandoned his

father's fine new city, and went back to Nineveh, which became the greatest capital that the Assyrian Empire was ever to know. His armies were all-powerful, his campaigns devastating —yet they were not his only concern. His mind was set on making of Nineveh the most beautiful city in the world, and he was critical of his near-ancestors' failure to have done so themselves. He said:

'Not one among them had given his thoughtful attention to, nor had his heart considered, the palace therein, the palace of the royal abode, the site of which had become too small; nor had he turned his thought, nor brought his mind, to lay out the streets of the city, to widen the squares, to dig a canal, or to set out trees.'

He was determined that Nineveh should be lapped in parkland and gardens and orchards; and he lost no time. Only a few years after his accession he said:

'A great part wherein were set out all kinds of herbs and orchard fruits, trees such as grow on the mountains and in Chaldea, I planted by the side of the Palace. That they might plant orchards, I divided some commonland above the city into plots for the citizens of Nineveh, and gave it to them. To make the orchards luxurious, from the border of the town of Kisiri to the plain about Nineveh, through mountain and lowland, with iron pickaxes I cut and directed a canal. I caused to flow everlasting waters from the Khosr. Inside those orchards I made them run in irrigation ditches.'

His greatest problem was the water supply. And he himself ranged far and wide into the foothills and mountains, searching out every stream and diverting its course, if he could, into the river Khosr, his men pick-axeing a way for the water through rocks in one place, and in another building up earthen banks to channel the flow. He said that he climbed Mount Musri in his search—and Mount Musri was none other than the green range, the Jebel Bashiqah, that ran just up there behind the house; he said, rather surprisingly for one so notoriously energetic (for its steep green slopes are no harder going than the highest of the South Downs), that he climbed it with much difficulty. Perhaps he was too used to the swift movement of a war chariot, as it bore him over the ground against some doomed Hebrew city. There went Sennacherib, a tiny figure striding along on the sky-line, followed probably by a trail of ministers and Court officials and engineers, sweating a little, but doing their best to keep up; while he nosed out water and yet more water for his beloved green city, careless of his father's mighty building lying just below him, already crumbling to decay. But as he planted out ever more land around Nineveh, setting it out with shrubs and rare trees and crops, he found that he must go deeper into the mountains to the east and compel far more water to his needs.

Jake had been told by a workman at Khorsabad the year before that there was a village in the mountains where the houses were partly built of great blocks of stone with writing on them. Jake listened idly, for archaeologists are used to being led for miles through rough country to see some marvellous inscription which turns out to be no more than a naturally scratched rough surface of rock. But this man had had the wit and the ability to make a sketch of some of the marks; he said they were on a stone which the owner of the house used as a seat outside the door. At this Jake became interested, for the signs on the paper were undoubtedly cuneiform. He made an expedition on donkey-back with Hussein, the workman. Through the pass beyond the house they went, on across a great plain to a little village called Ain Sifni; but Hussein did not stop there—he turned off to the right, south-easterly, and they went on for a few miles following a very rough road until they came into a valley through which a stream meandered. On the far side of the stream lay the village of Jerwan, built alongside a straight, grassy bank which ran at right angles to the stream, looking like part of a low, buried bridge.

The villagers were Yezidis, a strange sect of northerners speaking a dialect of Kurdish all their own; they have a wonderful shrine, fiercely cherished, up in the mountains a little beyond Ain Sifni. Jake was taken to see the Mukhtar, the Headman of the village, by Hussein, who luckily could speak the Yezidi dialect fairly well, and acted as interpreter. Ali the Mukhtar was sitting peacefully smoking outside his house, which was built up against the grass bank. He was sitting on a stone bench made of four great white blocks. The front of the blocks had inscriptions cut into them, just as Hussein had said; but they were only disappointing fragments. But when the old man got up to make greetings, Jake saw that there was a much fuller inscription, cut in a block in the wall against which the Mukhtar had been leaning. After an exchange of courtesies, Jake craned towards the wall; and on a stone built into this little thatched house in the quiet valley, nearly thirty miles from Nineveh, he read:

'Belonging to Sennacherib
King of the world, King of Assyria.'

"Where did this come from?" he asked.

"From the old dam outside—we have used its stone for many years."

Jake went and looked at the wide grass bank; it came to an end at the stream-bed and then clearly continued on the far side until it vanished into rising ground to the west. He asked if he could have a little of the grass and earth cleared from the vertical side of the bank; and the old man sent for a few villagers to cut away the turf. Soon white stone gleamed through the moist earth; and a clear-cut inscription ran along the finely cut face of the wall, to vanish behind the Mukhtar's house, which here met it at right angles. Jake brushed away the last of the turf and read the inscription as far as he could before it was concealed by the house:

'I caused to be dug . . .
Over deep-cut ravines a bridge
I spanned of white . . .
I caused to pass over upon it . . .'

He knew now that the grass-covered bank was a bridge of some kind, and not a dam—but what were the missing words? What had Sennacherib 'caused to pass over upon it'? His chariots? His armies? It was tantalising—and he very much wanted to find out. The Mukhtar took him back to his little house, all unaware that it was built of stone provided for him by the mightiest of the Assyrian Emperors, and gave him and Hussein bread to eat loaded with delicious curds and honey. He said again that the bank outside was a dam; it had been built by a king long, long ago to stem the flood-water from the mountains, so that the plain of Jerwan could be dried up and become pasture. Jake thought differently, but was much too busy trying to balance the curds and honey on the bread to do much arguing. Hans had agreed that it was well worth investigating; and now, this year, he and Rigmor and Seton were installed in a little thatched house in Ain Sifni, and were going to start the work of uncovering the mysterious structure in the remote valley at Jerwan.

Very late that night the guard reported a car coming along the road from Mosul—and soon afterwards it crawled up the ramp; and the Khafaje people crawled out. They had had a terrible journey—first through a heavy dust storm while they were in the train, and the rattling windows had kept none of it

167

at bay; and then through a downpour as they drove onwards. (Already this nightmare world which they were describing seemed unreal to me.) The driver had gone charging about over most of northern Iraq, they thought, searching out the driest tracks to follow. "And," said Betty, sinking whitefaced into a chair by the fire, with her hat tee'd up on her brow, "if anyone told me we'd got here by way of Chicago, I'd believe them." Pierre had wanted to stay in Mosul when at last they had reached it; but the others had insisted on doing the last fifteen miles out here, to die in comfort among friends. We rushed round with restoratives and soothing words, and they were soon blissfully happy, their troubles forgotten.

To this day I do not know what most of us were supposed to be doing that heavenly springtime at Khorsabad. Hans *did* want a high mound called Shenshi investigated, a little way along the road; and Pierre and Mac and Hal went dutifully off every day and investigated it—but, in my totally irresponsible frame of mind just then, I never took in what they were supposed to be at, and it's just a question if they did either. It began, disconcertingly, on the very top with an old, old cemetery. Hal told me that all he did was to climb up to the top of Shenshi every morning, and walk round and round it smiling gently at the view, occasionally tripping over a skeleton.

Ham was helping Gordon with his surveying, but if come upon unexpectedly was usually doing it flat on his back in the grass with a cigarette, smiling gently at the sky. He would say that, like Hyman Kaplan, he was doing some 'dip t'inkink'. Rachel and Betty vaguely helped Gordon with registration and domestic chores, and Hans tried to send coherent reports to Chicago; while I did practically nothing, and developed a technique, which has never since deserted me, of managing to look extremely busy in the process. Occasionally, with the bribe of a Dutch cheroot, Hans suggested that I might type something for him. Nobody worried—and Gordon bore the invasion of his peace indulgently, and produced incredibly good American meals; in between which we kept our figures by ranging far and wide over the countryside. Sometimes we strode along the great skyline of Sennacherib's Mount Musri, along a prehistoric track which Hans showed us. Up here we could now see right across the great plain eastwards to Ain Sifni; and here, too, we had an unbroken view of the great snow-covered mountain ranges stretching as far as the eye could see north and south, and far away into the hinterland of Kurdistan and Persia. Sometimes we kept to the plain, discovering enchanting villages sheltering beneath the looming downland; little villages shaded by real trees—never palms up here—where clear water bubbled everywhere along raised stone channels, and shy, smiling Kurds greeted us, and where through a doorway in a stone wall you might catch a sudden glimpse of a small garden full of roses. We would pass great rain-pools in the grassland, where storks waded; they were nesting now in the tall trees at Khorsabad village, and beat slowly to and fro between their home and the water, un-hurried, unfrightened. The old black spaniel belonging to the dig would rush into the shallows, barking at them; they would simply fly up out of reach for a few moments as he came bounding and splashing, lazily retracting their dangling legs just enough to clear his waving ears; and as he shot beneath them, looking surprised at having somehow missed fire ("Dash it! I *know* there were storks here!"), they would quietly let themselves down again into the water behind him, and go peacefully on with their own affairs, while he shook himself all over us, and expected to be called a very, very clever dog.

A message came from Ain Sifni one day that Hans was urgently required there; he set out in the dig car very early the next morning and it didn't take a Dutch cheroot to persuade me to go too. The track from Ain Sifni to Jerwan was very rough for a car, and we pitched and tossed over boulders and across the beds of several wadis, almost dry now. Then we came to the valley.

"*Mon Dieu!*" Hans murmured as we approached the village. "How much they have done since I was here."

There they were, waiting for us—Seton, thinner than ever, with his amused, twisted smile beneath his dark glasses. Jake in khaki shirt and shorts, hair bleached almost white in the sun— and Rigmor, brown as a berry and radiant. There was a look of suppressed triumph about them. All round, Yezidi workmen were moving the earth away from the dig, while a few Shergatis that Seton had brought along were tapping at the sides of the stone walls. The Yezidis were fiercely gay in scarlet headcloths and white shirts and baggy trousers. They wore their hair long, either hanging loose to the shoulder, or braided in several tight little greasy plaits. There was no touch of blue anywhere in their clothes; for Shaitan (Satan), whom they propitiate, is offended by the colour.

All the turf had gone from the top and from part of the sides of the bridge which stretched white and clear on either side of the stream. They told us that it was more than 900 feet long over all. We walked to the great gap where the little stream trickled through, and Seton showed us that the bed of the river here had once been paved to take the weight of arches which spanned it. On one side of the stream he had found two of the pointed arches almost intact, and in the bed of the stream a heavy semi-circular breakwater, inscribed, on which the pier of an arch had rested. The river then must have run deep and wide and strong for there to be need of such impressively sturdy breakwaters. Seton had calculated from the curve of the surviving arches and the distance to be spanned that there must have been five originally, and after taking some measurements had moved across to the level turf on the other side of the river-bed, and indicated to a few workmen an exact spot to dig down through the soil, telling them that about two metres below they would find a rounded stone with writing on it. They must have credited him with magical power when their picks came down plumb on the fifth breakwater exactly where he had said.

The remains of low parapets could be seen here and there along the sides of the bridge; and between them the surface had been made of paving-stones laid very carefully over a deep layer of concrete. Jake and Seton said that they had found the immense care with which the surface had been treated very mystifying—until the day before. Then, in clearing down the north side of the bridge, just opposite Mukhtar Ali's house, Seton had revealed several fine buttresses, and on each of them, and on each recess between, a finely cut cuneiform inscription.

"Come and see it, Hans," said Jake.

We all moved along the northern side of the bridge, until Jake stopped at one bay where the inscription was very clear.

"The same inscription is repeated, all along the wall," he said. "And what I saw in the wall by Ali's house last year is part of it."

"Go on," said Hans.

Jake read slowly from the white blocks of stone, emphasising as he came to them, the words already known from Ali's fragment:

" 'Sennacherib, King of the world, King of Assyria, says: For a long distance, adding to it the waters of the springs of the mountains to the right and left at its sides, *I caused to be dug* a canal to the meadows of Nineveh. *Over deep-cut ravines a bridge I spanned of white* stone blocks. *I caused to pass over upon it*—those waters.' "

Water. Not chariots. Not armies.

There was a short silence. Then Hans turned to look down the great shining length of white stonework as it stretched away over the grass.

" 'I caused to pass over upon it *those waters,*' " he repeated, shaking his head a little as he sometimes did when words were inadequate. "Then it is an aqueduct—the oldest aqueduct ever known."

.   .   .   .   .   .

At the midday break we walked a little way up the valley and had a picnic in the grass by the stream, where a small humped bridge crossed it. Blue drifts of a kind of large speed-well shone along the edges of the water, and small moist ferns trembled and sparkled among tiny waterfalls. And in the grass there were little pink and mauve orchis flowers, and ruffled tulips streaked red and yellow, and everywhere anemones swayed in the gentle breeze, white and blue and dark purple and blazing scarlet. The Yezidis hang scarlet anemones over the doorway of their shrine, for it is the blood of the dying god Adonis, and his cult is woven deep into the rich strange fabric of their worship.

"We must try and trace the route of the canal," said Hans, thoughtfully biting into a large sandwich.

"I think at the eastern end of the aqueduct the canal proper begins to swing round the hill to the north into the next valley," said Seton. "The Gomel river runs down that valley."

"Then probably he diverted that river into the canal some-where up the valley—we must investigate it when you have finished here."

Jake began to tell us a folk-tale that a chance word had brought to light among the workmen during the last few days. It was an old, a very old story, which all the unlettered Yezidis of Jerwan, and some of the villagers of Ain Sifni knew. We lay among the flowers, with the water rippling by, while Jake, pulling at his curly Danish pipe, began in his gentle Danish voice, like a modern Hans Andersen:

"Once upon a time, long long ago, there was a King with a beautiful daughter. And the King needed much water for his city to make it fair and green. And the daughter had two suitors, one of whom she loved. And the King said that he would give the Princess to that one who could bring water to his city to make it fair and green. One suitor at once went away and set to work in the hills and mountains far from the city; and he dug canals and brought the water nearer and nearer to the city. But the second suitor, whom the Princess loved, sat idle in the coffeehouse. And when the first suitor had brought the water nearly to the city, the second went out and fetched very many linen sheets, and spread them on the ground at night close to the city wall. And when the sun came up and shone upon the linen, it seemed as water; and the first suitor seeing it from afar believed that the other had fulfilled the task; and he died of grief. And the other suitor won the Princess."

Down there below us, Sennacherib's aqueduct stretched across the grass. The workmen were resting in little groups, perched about on its stones, the Yezidis' head-shawls gleaming as bright as their own scarlet anemones. They had never known that the grassy bank, which they called a dam, had once carried water across the valley—and yet, Sennacherib's tremendous exploit still lived on in their memory, fairy-tale fashion, handed down to them by word of mouth, over a span of more than 2600 years.

.   .   .   .   .   .

A few days after this Hans left for Amsterdam, where he was lecturing before going on to England for his usual rich summer of work and music and books and art exhibitions and gardening and friends and then more work again. It would be a heavy summer in the office, for everything that we had done, and everything that we had found at Tell Asmar, Khafaje, Khorsabad and now Jerwan (even Shenshi, perhaps, skeletons and all, would have its little memorial notice slipped in somewhere), had to be co-ordinated and prepared for publication. Now that I was rested, it was good to know that, as I had followed Hans up here out of the dust storms, so I would soon be following in his wake to London; for wherever Hans was, life was rich and stimulating. Trying to keep up with him became the normal pattern of my days and a major preoccupation, in more ways than one, from now on; whether I was knitting my brows over railway and ship time-tables as I shuttled between London and Baghdad year after year, following my leader; or over the absorbing close-woven fabric of his articles and essays and lectures and books. His writings were hard going for one who had no basic scholarship, but infinitely rewarding for the effort. And he was always ready to explain. Complex and brilliant as he was, he suffered the ignorant—but never fools—perhaps not gladly, but at least gently, so long as they were humble about it, and tried really hard to use what brains they had; but the pompous ignorant he flayed, and was thought by such to be arrogant.

Khorsabad now—London soon. Life was very good—and seemed near perfect when a letter came from the Pendleburys suggesting that I—and Seton too if he could come—should spend a few weeks in Crete with them before going on to England. I caught a faint echo from a year back—John calling from the quay at Piraeus: "Crete next year"—the magic circle was nearly complete.

But before we left Khorsabad, our work in Iraq that season was rounded off with an unexpected flourish. Gordon had a telegram from Baghdad to say that King Feisal was coming north on holiday, and wanted to see the dig—particularly the new cherubim—and would arrive at midday in two days' time. The Crown Prince would be with him, and the party would number about twelve. We thought it was lovely until we noticed Gordon's face. It was a wonderful study of combined frenzy and panic and amusement—chiefly frenzy.

"Those goddam bulls," he said. "The men finished burying them again to-day—it's cost nearly a week's money."

He tottered off to put all the men he could back on to the job of unburying the bulls at top speed, and then cleaning them till they shone; and as the two great heads broke surface for the second time that season, their smiles seemed broader than before. "Here we go again," they seemed to say. "Have done with your picks and shovels and brooms, little men. Leave us now to shine in the sun forever while we protect our King— for we are the King's Beasts."

The rest of us rushed about in preparation, arguing about procedure as we went. Mac said we could all bow and curtsey till we were dizzy as far as he was concerned, but *he'd* been brought up not to believe in kings, and on principle he'd be darned if *he* was going to bow.

The morning of the visit came, and towards noon a shout went up from the guard whom Gordon had stationed as a look-out on the top of Sargon's ziggurat. We all ran to the western edge of the mound. Very far away, just clear of the green walls of Nineveh, a long line of cars was moving along Sargon's road. As it came nearer, we could see an escort of Arab horsemen riding grandly on either side of the first car. White robes and headshawls shone, scarlet and green and gold harness tassels tossed, sword-hilts and rifle-barrels flashed. The horsemen didn't ride in formal escort, but whirled and circled in the fields by the roadside like great white gulls, wild and graceful, wheeling round a convoy of small ships that pitched and tossed a little through choppy water. The cars slowed, turned, and one by one mounted the ramp. Out of the first car stepped King Feisal and the Crown Prince Ghazi. Once again a King with his young heir had come up from Nineveh.

But here was a man of peace, his fighting days behind him. It was many years now since, with Lawrence, he had secured Allenby's right flank and rolled up the Turkish army as far as Damascus and beyond. He was tall and slim; a fine head, with grizzled hair growing back from a noble forehead above tired, very shrewd hazel eyes. It was plain to see why Lawrence knew at first meeting that this was the man he sought as leader of the fighting Arabs.

'I felt at first glance that this was the man I had come to Arabia to seek—the leader who would bring the Arab Revolt to full glory. Feisal looked very tall and pillar-like, very slender, in his long white silk robes and his brown headcloth bound with a brilliant scarlet and gold cord. His eyelids were dropped; and his black beard and colourless face were like a mask against the strange, still watchfulness of his body. His hands were crossed in front of him on his dagger.'

He shook us all by the hand, and Mac with tremendous dignity bowed deeper over that hand than anybody. He said afterwards: "He sure was my idea of a King."

We lunched out of doors on the wide grass ledge overlooking Sargon's Throne Room. Rachel sat on Feisal's right, I on his left; opposite us Betty and the Crown Prince, a slim, shy, smiling youth in trim uniform, just home from school at Harrow. So King Feisal sat and talked with us, eyes roaming now over the long hall where King Sargon had once sat and given audience, now lifting with a curious look of longing to the hills just beyond, where King Sennacherib had once climbed. After lunch he asked to be shown all over the dig, and then the quiet, rather frail-looking man became transformed with a sort of electric energy. He went everywhere, with long, quick strides, looking at everything, asking innumerable questions. Young Prince Ghazi, a head shorter than his father, was on the run most of the time; and after them trailed the ministers and Court officials, sweating a little, but doing their best to keep up. . . .

After it was all over at the end of the afternoon, Ham and Hal and I went for a walk to the hills. As evening fell, we came back through a little village. Ahead of us a Kurdish peasant, dark ringlets falling to his shoulders from under a turban set at a rakish angle, was walking home with a large Nanny-goat anxiously trotting at his heels, first to one side of him, then to the other. Every time she bleated, this fierce-looking man answered her in a sort of crooning reassuring murmur. As we caught up with him we saw that he was carrying very gently a newborn, silky-eared kid. The man greeted us with a smile as he reached his house and turned to slip through the doorway. Blue smoke drifted up from the cluster of little houses. Against the flaming sunset the dark mass of Sargon's citadel loomed above us like the sinister threat which it once had been to half the known world.

But Nahum had long been avenged. The old lion was gone, and the old lion's whelp, Sennacherib; Nineveh was laid waste.

The country was at peace, and a good man was King.

CHAPTER NINE

FIVE RUBIES, STRUNG on an invisible thread across a black world, glowed in the night ahead of us. Every now and then one or two would vanish; sometimes they would all dwindle to pin-pricks far, much too far away. Rachel and I were in the last car of a convoy struggling westwards from Mosul to the northern railway terminus at Nisibin in north-east Syria. The Macs were in one of the cars ahead. The country out here, the most northerly part of Iraq, quite near to the hilly Turkish frontier, was very desolate—a treeless, rolling plain with nothing but a rutted track full of pot-holes winding up hill and down dale across it, endlessly. Yet, for all its seeming emptiness, the plain was the home of the Yezidi people, many of them doubtless going about their lawful occasions peacefully; but the reputation they had gained for banditry was such that the authorities frowned on those who travelled this road alone; and they went at their own risk. The normal way was by convoy—which seemed to me a first-class idea if you happened to be in any car but the last one. I could not help wondering— between bouts of slight concussion, as I caught my head crack after crack on the roof or the window-frame—what happened if the last car broke down, which this one showed every sign of doing. In the black night no one in front would ever know. The weather had changed; the sky was heavy with cloud, the track deep in wet mud. We bucketed along, slithering and plunging; sometimes we slowed to a standstill, with spinning wheels and grunting driver; and then the five little lights would draw further and further away, perhaps to vanish altogether in a distant dip, or round a hill. Then we would churn into life again, lurch on down the track, and after an uncomfortably nervous mile or two, thankfully catch sight again of the last red light, and then another and another. The Old Superb had absolutely nothing on us when it came to lame ducks lagging, lagging all the way. It's all a case of keeping together, I thought hazily, watching the lights in the dark; happy times shouldn't end, shouldn't come apart.

Gordon had driven us in to Mosul at sunset; and the convoy had left the Rest House at midnight. It had rained at Khorsabad all day; but the sun had shone out again, low and level, from beneath a long black cloud, just as the car moved down the ramp. The old brown house suddenly turned golden, and against the purple-clouded hills the whiteness of a stork, beating slowly over the house towards the pools, flushed to deep rose as the long fingers of the sun touched its feathers.

Ham and Hal stood alone at the top of the ramp as we left.

"See you in London," I'd said, laughing and casual.

"See you in London," answered my dear friends; and I knew the small death of leaving a fragment of life behind that would never come again, however good the future might be.

．　　．　　．　　．　　．　　．

That drive went on for eleven hours. At last the chilly light of dawn strengthened behind us, and each time that we opened heavy eyes between uneasy dozes, the world had grown brighter, the plain greener.

"I don't think I shall ever be warm again," Rachel murmured miserably from her corner.

It was a little better when the sun came up; but we were desperately tired and shaken. Then in the middle of the morning the cars ahead trailed up a slight slope and vanished one by one through a gap on the low sky-line, as they seemed to have

179

done a hundred times before. We followed; and, as we cleared the gap, looked down on a wonderfully odd sight. The monotonous green landscape still lay before us—but at last it was not quite empty. The cars were dropping down the slope towards something tiny and square and black, standing all by itself in the plain. Stretching away on the far side of it, a gleaming double thread ran towards the far horizon. We were looking at the buffers which marked the end of a run—unbroken except for the water-jump at Stamboul—which had begun more than 2000 miles away, where the great Simplon–Orient–Express draws away from the salty grey waves that lap the old harbour wall at Calais.

It looked unreal—as if a baby giant had set up his toy rails and buffers on an infinite nursery floor. And now far off a model train came sliding along, slowing to a crawl as it reached its journey's end—bonk! against the lonely little buffers in the middle of nowhere. As the small, shattered herd of travellers crept out of the cars and waited, drooping in the sunshine, while luggage was unroped and stacked beside them, the last incongruous touch materialised in the shape of a homunculus in trim brown uniform, peaked cap and gleaming buttons, a French-speaking wagon-lit attendant, who jumped down the high steps of the sleeping-car, and welcomed us aboard. Rachel and I smiled wanly at the Macs, and disappeared into the haven of our sleeper, and in a second passed from one world to another, dazed amongst the solid comfort of cushioned seats, surrounded by gleaming dark wood, winking brass and glass, spotless towels and running water. We asked the little man to make up the beds right away, and just managed to stay awake until he had gone; and never stirred, never even knew that the rumbling, grumbling wheels had begun to turn beneath us, when the train drew away late in the afternoon on the long lap to Stamboul.

The Lion Gate of Mycenae,
entrance to the Fortress
of Agamemnon

The Theatre at Epidaurus.

John Pendlebury in Crete.

Flowery Milatos.

Cretan family.

It took two nights and two days to slant across north-westerly from the eastern frontier of Syria to Stamboul. Early the next morning we were rounding the corner of the Mediterranean, where Syria meets Turkey. Then we turned inland, heading for the great range of the Taurus Mountains, and began to weave very slowly this way and that along its southern rocky slopes, in long, steep gradients. By the evening we were high up, crawling broadside on to the way we had come. Below us a great rock barrier cut across the huge coastal plain, dividing the mountains sharply from the low ground beyond. But there was one clear-cut square gap in it, a wide nick in the long range, which had been channelled out through the ages by the river flowing through it and away to the blue distance. This gap was the Cilician Gates, through which Alexander had passed with his great army towards Antioch and Arbil and the East. Beyond the plain we could see right across the blue corner of the sea which we had curved round so many hours before, and beyond the water the far mountains of Syria, snow-capped, flushed in the setting sun. Then the train turned away from the plain for the last time, and plunged into the heart of the mountains, and began to gather speed, for we had reached the top of the climb. We shot in and out of brief tunnels, flickering in and out of the twilight, now a flashing glimpse of stupendous grey peaks soaring above us, now of dizzily deep canyons, as we rocked along a narrow ledge; then again a roaring blackness, as we burrowed into the mountain. Down we dropped all that night—and the next day is a gentle memory all the way of lovely valleys filled with the white and pink of foaming blossom, and of streams winding in clean, stony beds until, as daylight faded again, we slid quietly to a standstill on the shores of the Bosphorus at Scutari.

A nautical Thomas Cook in oilskins shepherded us out of the station after a while into several small launches to cross the water. It was quite dark now, and at first nothing could be seen of Stamboul except for a few twinkling lights, some high up, tangled with the stars. A naked electric bulb over T. Cook's head glared in our faces and lit the bobbing water. "You like to see Old Stamboul?" he asked, as we peered ahead in vain. He put up a long arm and unfixed the bulb, and we were suddenly in the dark. But now we could see the land—two long, high hills linked just ahead of us by a row of lights at water level.

"Old Stamboul," said Thomas, pointing to the hill on the left of the bridge. On its crest, silhouetted black against the deep blue, star-sprinkled sky, lay a fairy-land of crowding domes and towers and soaring minarets.

"The Golden Horn," he went on, pointing at the bridge. "The water runs inland there a long way, between the two cities, the Old and the New."

We bumped gently against a wooden landing-stage, and a moment later were standing on a piece of Europe again.

For two days we drifted about the mosques and Bazaar and Palace of old Stamboul; and then Rachel left on a train for Calais; and the familiar dig refrain: "See you in London," sounded once more. That evening I boarded a ship for Athens, and: "See you in Syria," called the Macs, laughing among the crowd on the quay, for they would be digging near Aleppo next season.

I waved till I couldn't see them any longer, and then leaned on the rail, a lone traveller once more, as the ship slid slowly past the wonderful old city. High up there, in the Palace of the Sultans, I'd seen their fabulous riches, their carpets worked in pearls and precious stones of every colour—the largest emerald in the world suspended on a thin chain over a jewel-encrusted throne—room after room where walls and pillars were covered with priceless sets of china—a tiny golden reading-desk for the little son of a mighty ruler, where even the letter-pointer was of solid gold finished off at the end with a blazing diamond. Up there I had wandered through paved courtyards and into little tree-shaded pavilions; from the ship I could see now, high on the eastern corner of the ancient walls, the little polygonal room, all blue-tiled inside, named the Baghdad Pavilion, where the Sultan could sit, gazing through its fretted windows across the water towards his distant lands. And standing up there myself, looking out over the Bosphorus across to Turkey-in-Asia, I'd thought back along that journey so burningly clear in my mind, all the way back to distant Baghdad; crowding memories of fresh-seen beauty and strange places; of tough travelling and unbelievable fatigue; of swiftly returning energy when the hard moments passed. And coupled with this was another journey that I'd travelled these last six months—one of wider knowledge and deeper experience, and an awakened curiosity to know much more; here's richness, I thought, to carry away with me, enough to dim all the swinging emeralds and jewelled carpets in the world.

The prow of the ship began to cleave the darkening waters more swiftly now, and the rigging began to hum in a strengthening breeze; we were out in mid-stream, heading for the Sea of Marmora; and soon the dreaming walls and domes and minarets had faded away, sunk into a faint blur on the dark hills astern. I turned to look forward, south-westerly; in a few hours we would pass through the narrows into the Aegean, where somewhere far away to the south, lay Crete.

·   ·   ·   ·   ·   ·

The next morning I reached Athens, and found Rosaleen waiting for me in a hotel. She was coming to Crete, too—she had been at Amarna the year before, helping in the work. Her assistance took various forms, for while she cleaned an antiquity here, or mended a pot there, she was usually also at the receiving end of somebody's life-story—for she was the world's best listener. Small and quiet and poised, with red-gold hair; a gleaming Irish blue eye and a gleaming Irish wit kept strictly in hand beneath an exquisitely demure manner.

I disentangled her from a gentleman in the lounge—who was telling her his life-story—and we went round to a shipping office in Syntagma Square, and found that there was a boat leaving for Crete late in the afternoon. We booked a cabin.

"I hope it's a nice big boat," I said to the very young Greek clerk. "The weather doesn't look too good."

"Not so big," he said sadly, and named an alarmingly low tonnage. Then he peered through the window at the blue-and-white flag on the Parliament Building opposite. It was flat out, streaming away from the quivering flagstaff. "I wouldn't like to cross in her myself tonight. But she'll *get* there all right," he added briskly, suddenly remembering his salesmanship.

We crept out. It takes fourteen long hours to get to Crete in a small boat, and I am a nervous sailor. In the afternoon we taxied down the four miles to Piraeus, and as we came in sight of the sea, noticed, as expected, and with a sinking feeling, that there was a fine lop on the grey waters, even in the harbour, and that the sea beyond was all flecked with white. We drove slowly round the quay, looking for Xanthippe, inspecting the sterns backed against the quayside, for all the crowded shipping was packed side by side, pointing outwards. Then I read across one rusty-looking stern "X A N T . . . ." and said to Rosaleen: "Here she is—and not really so small, after all." We stopped the taxi; and as we got out, Xanthippe seemed to split lengthways, and one half slid quietly away into the open harbour. I saw that my optimism about her width had been premature—she was only the tiny bit that had been left behind. Full of foreboding, we picked our way over ropes and rings, through groups of patient peasants squatting on the deck amid sacks and bundles of clothes and tall wicker baskets full of vegetables and oranges, and found our way below to the miniature cabin. Not long afterwards we moved off, heading south for the open sea. The little boat seemed wonderfully steady, and hope revived—perhaps, in spite of the wind and the white horses, we should somehow have a good crossing, after all. The evening wore on and darkness fell swiftly; and at the sound of a gong, the few cabin passengers gathered in the little dining-saloon, nearly the width of the boat. There was a definite movement now, and I looked unhappily at my soup, which was making frantic efforts to climb out of the bowl.

"Well, if it doesn't get any worse than this——" Rosaleen began to say, and the soup suddenly shot across the table, and we all fell out of our chairs. Somehow we got back to the cabin.

The reason for the comparative calm till that moment was that we had still been running in the shelter of the long arm of the Argolid, which stretches southward for miles—but once clear of its southern tip we first met the westerly wind full, broadside on, and a little later the tumbling waters racing before it through the channel between the mainland and Crete. All night we hung on to the edges of our bunks and listened to the waves smacking and thundering against the cabin wall—so loud that it seemed as if the frail shell could not withstand the buffeting much longer; but the little ship wallowed gamely on.

When at last I could see daylight through the streaming porthole, I put on a coat and staggered up on deck; and in the sparkling air the misery of the night was swept away in a twinkling. The sky was luminous and cloudless, the sun just up. Looking towards the splendid sunrise, the leaping seas against it were inky black; but when I looked westward, where the sun was striking strong and level on the racing waves, they were all crimson, laced with gold, and the swirling, shifting troughs shimmered peacock-blue and jade.

And there ahead, not many miles distant, stretching away on either side of the plunging bows, rose a high range of purple mountains, majestical, magnificently still in a rocking world.

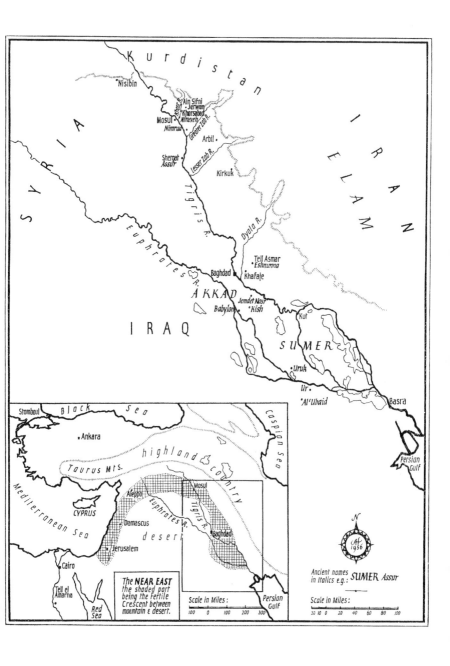

CHAPTER TEN

KNOSSOS, THE PALACE of Minos, lies about three miles inland
—that is, south—from Candia, the capital of Crete. It lies to one
side of the modern highway running north and south across the
island, which follows the ancient trade route towards the harbour nearest to the Egyptian coast. The remains of the Palace
are spread wide over a low hilltop, a hill formed of earlier
crumbled Palaces, and below them settlements of Early
Minoan and Neolithic times, dating back more than 1000
years before the time when the strange king, known as Minos,
himself ruled here about 1400 B.C. The hill is dwarfed by the
great mountains which look down on the lovely valley where
Knossos lies. The Villa Ariadne, the Cretan home of Sir Arthur
Evans, lay on the hillside on the other side of the road, hidden
among trees; and on that April day when Rosaleen and I drove
up from the sea it was smothered in great, warm-scented sprays
and bushes of honeysuckle spilling over the terrace and steps
and paths. The white, dusty road winding up from the harbour
looked as though it had been made ready for a royal procession
—for banks of flowers crowded thick along the verges and
over the low stone walls beyond, great yellow marguerites and
crimson campion, wild gladioli and anemones and rock-roses.

Sir Arthur Evans was in England at this time, and John, who
as Curator was at the moment in sole charge, had just finished
the excavation of a Royal tomb near the Palace.

"When will Seton get here?" he asked, when we had settled
down and recounted our adventures—the floor was still rocking a little underfoot.

"He hoped to follow in about a week," I said. "But when last heard of was heading towards Persia. It all depends on how much water Sennacherib found in the Gomel river—if he didn't find enough we may never see Seton again. He will just go on and on and on into the mountains."

John suggested gently that I explain what I was talking about; so I told them about the aqueduct.

"Then that will give you a week to get to know the Palace a bit," he said. "We'll wait for him before we start walking. I want to do a walk towards the east—quite a gentle one," he added for Rosaleen's benefit, who wasn't sure of her walking capacity, but was willing to try anything once.

As yet we had only had a glimpse of the Palace hill, for it lies a little beyond the Villa Ariadne, and slightly below the road, screened by a grove of trees; a week seemed a longish time to "get to know the Palace a bit"; and I still thought so when we dipped down off the road the next morning and then wound up through spice-scented trees, blowing in a warm south wind, to the great, empty, sun-soaked area at the top of the hillock. But Knossos, even in fragments, still hides a thousand secrets; and I soon realised that in a week one could only begin to absorb the vast and complicated plan of its latest building, quite apart from understanding the earlier structures, or distinguishing the myriad details which had provided the evidence for all the reconstruction which Sir Arthur Evans had carried out.

The first thing that John showed us was the smudged signs of fire running all along the first long western wall we came to, and the marks where a burning beam must have crashed down from a ceiling and rested in flames against the wall.

"The Palace was finally destroyed mainly by fire, about 1400 B.C." he said. "Probably late in April."

"But how *can* you tell the time of year?" Rosaleen asked wonderingly.

"Or perhaps early in May," he said. "Feel the wind now."

It was blowing hard up the valley from the south.

"Just at this time of year it blows always just from that direction," he said. "Look at this wall—quite white and clean to the south of the beam; all the marks of burning run along it northward."

We asked about the destruction of the Palace, and he explained how gradually the great sea-kings of Crete, sometime after 2000 B.C., had become very powerful and dominated the mainland of Greece. Their trade, particularly with Egypt, had brought them the mastery of the eastern Mediterranean. The fact that the Palace was without any system of fortification showed how secure the Cretans felt in their sea-power. Yet, as the years of their high and lovely civilisation sped on, a danger, unknown to them at first, was looming to north and east; for waves of new people, adventurous and questing, were pressing down into the mainland of Greece and Asia Minor from the vast lands beyond, until they reached the shores and gazed with wonder at the great sea to the south. The Dorians filtered into the islands of the Aegean—and as they grew in strength and found the ability to organise that strength, and as they learned to pass safely over the dancing waters, so were the days of Crete's glory numbered. Sometime about 1400 B.C.—in the late spring (which is the time of year that legend has it Theseus set sail from Athens to slay the Minotaur)—the end came in fire and blood, not only for proud Knossos, but also for many of the lovely cities all over the island.

John said that he believed you could find the germ of true fact in the story of Theseus coming to rescue the noble youths and maidens who sailed each year from Athens as dreadful tribute to the devouring Minotaur, the Bull of Minos. Every child knows how the young hero destroyed the monster with the help of Ariadne; how she gave him a scarlet thread which brought him safely out of the dark maze of the lair.

"You know about the Cretan sport of bull-leaping, don't you?" he said. "Young men—and girls, too—stood in the arena while the bull came at them; as he lowered his horns for the toss, they seized them and hung on; and as the bull's head came up they were spun over in a backward somersault, and landed feet foremost on his back; and then jumped to the ground. Horribly difficult and dangerous—and there *must* have been plenty of fatalities. I've an idea that the youths and maidens came voluntarily to compete in annual games; and the fact that many of the young men, the flower of the mainland youth, can never have survived the games to become soldiers or leaders of soldiers, must have suited Cretan policy very nicely. It would be quite natural, I think, as the story of that long-ago victory over Crete was handed down, generation after generation, gathering folk-tale embroidery as it went, for the idea of the fabulously powerful island king to become fused with the faint memory of a savage bull who destroyed their young people. And the legendary hero, Theseus, would symbolise for them the whole great movement when their mainland ancestors rose against Crete, and left its cities in flames."

The bull motif was everywhere, for as we turned the corner of the wall and began to mount a flight of shallow steps into a graceful portico, we could see that the parapets were decorated with bulls' horns carved in stone. On the inner wall of the porch was a coloured frieze—a procession of kilted young men, lifesize, carrying different shaped vases. Broad of shoulder, very slim of waist, with curly heads flung backward and tucked-in chins—Ham would have made a very good Cretan, I thought.

"Minos might even have worn a crown with bull's horns," John went on. "If so it would be an added reason for the legend of a horrifying enthroned monster—think of a young Greek warrior, sword drawn, storming through the smoke-filled passages to find him, at bay, a great, horned, crouching figure in the darkened Throne Room."

"Do you know where the Throne Room was?" I asked.

"Come on," he said in answer. We came on; almost trotting, which we knew from experience in Egypt was the normal way you assimilated archaeology in John's company.

North of the portico we dived into a maze of dark corridors, and courtyards and rooms, and became utterly bewildered, as John wove this way and that, through ancient doorways, up and over huge stone blocks, past pillared light-wells. Some of it was underground.

"I'll give you the plan to bring round with you next time—once you have the plan clear it's much easier to follow, not to mention explain."

We passed from a great open courtyard into a small, shadowy room, with a doorway on the far side opening into a room that was even darker.

"This is the anteroom to the Throne Room," John said; and although he spoke levelly, there was a hint of excitement in his voice, as if, used though he was to this place, he could never enter it without hearing a faint distant clamour, a ringing of sword against dagger blade, a crackling of flames.

We crossed the room and went through the narrow doorway beyond. There was no need for him to say anything. Against the right-hand wall stood a stone seat with a high, curved back. The Throne of Minos.

"It stands there just as it was found," John said quietly. "And there were vessels lying about on the floor, and an overturned oil-jar."

The scene seemed to grow up out of the shadows as we stood there. Here in this narrow doorway, on just such a day of sun and wind more than 3000 years ago, a young Greek chieftain may have stood, panting a little, his short sword crimson at the point, wary, poised for a moment before moving in to the kill, towards the proud and desperate figure looming up from the Throne.

In the sun again, John led us up to a room above, where copies of frescoes found in different parts of the Palace were hung behind glass. The originals are preserved for greater safety in the museum at Candia. There was the magnificent bull-leaping fresco, the huge beast charging at full gallop, one athlete clinging to the horns and already well off the ground in the first upward rush; another, locks streaming, whirling over the bull's back; and a third, triumphant, poised, hands outstretched to catch his friend as he lands. Here, too, were pictures of the crowds watching the games: a mass of little faces and figures drawn in black line on washes of different colour, dark red for a group of men and patches of white for the women, who sat eagerly chattering in pretty full-skirted dresses, flaunting ringlets like early Victorians.

We crossed the site until we were standing on the eastern edge of the hillock; it fell here quite steeply to a long, green, level strip of grass. On the further side a small river twinkled along among trees, and beyond that the ground rose up steeply, high above us, into a grey-green rocky range.

"We think that the bull-leaping took place just down there," said John. "It's a perfect place for an arena—the only level piece of ground anywhere near."

Just below us, perhaps, on seats backed against the eastern wall of the Palace, and there opposite, along the river-side, the slim, sunburned Cretans had sat with their fair ladies in ringlets and crinolines, the air humming with their chatter and laughter; the hubbub dying away suddenly to a tense silence as one of the athletes ran out to take his place, a lonely figure, there on the grass below. Soon the silence is broken by the sound of swift hooves—there he comes, tawny-red against the grass, head down, straight for the willowy young figure. The boy leans forward now, hands ready, braced for the shock; death is certain if the wicked horns slip past his hands. Then the air cracks as a great shout bursts from the crowd—he is up, carried backward in the mad rush. But the horns are held firm in his hands—for a moment he swings lightly between them; then the great head, with bellowing mouth, tosses upward furiously, to be rid of the dangling impish burden; the slim legs fly up, the boy balances for a second on his hands; then his feet sink over his head, disdainfully he casts away the horns behind him, bounces upright for a moment on the broad back and then skips over the tail to the ground. The mob-howl of excitement mingled with terror softens to warm applause and laughter and hand-clapping.

The week slipped away. We went back again and again to the Palace, drawn by its complex mystery; and it seemed to grow larger every time—until at last we began to recognise the turns and twists of the shadowy passages, and know that, here, this colonnaded outer hall would lead to another decorated with replicas of the huge ox-hide shields which once had hung here; and that, there, that door would lead into a narrow corridor towards the Queen's apartments. Here in one airy room, where once she had sat with her ladies, the walls were decorated with gay blue dolphins and fishes and sea-urchins; at Knossos you could never forget for long that you were near the sea. Not far from this room is the most wonderful feature of the whole Palace. Round the sides of a deep light-well the Grand Staircase rises in wide flights of shallow steps up to the open central court. It is not only marvellous that such a thing could have been constructed so beautifully at such an early date; it is the wonderful skill of Sir Arthur Evans in preserving it—for as he dug down through the collapsed rubble, each step had to be strengthened or rebuilt in concrete before he could safely remove the supporting earth beneath it.

Sometimes we found our way about the Palace in the moonlight—it was strange to move alone along the eerie corridors, cross a silver river barred with the slanting shadows of an open colonnade, on into some mysterious hall, with a glimpse, perhaps, of a far-away moonlit hill framed in a black doorway. A nearby footfall, or low voices, would startle me—and groping round a corner into the Queen's Megaron, I would find Hilda and Rosaleen murmuring in the slanting moonbeams, not the crinolined ladies I had half expected to see—or beyond, moving silently up the Grand Staircase, in and out of the moonlight, not the ghost of a young Cretan officer of the guard on his nightly rounds, but John, slim in white flannels, flitting lightly through his beloved Palace whose safe-keeping was now in his sole care. And all the while nightingales filled the warm air with a never-ending sweetness.

We made short expeditions across the island by car, and along the coast to the west, bathing and picnicking and lazing, and looking at other lovely, confusing sites sprawling under the pine-scented trees. One such along the northern coast was Tylissos; but all I remember of it is that in the nearby village a certain Domenico Theotokopuli was born, who is never called by any other name but his nickname of 'The Greek'— El Greco.

Sometimes we played with David, rising two and intensely active—and who can wonder? He was usually pulling strongly at the front end of long reins, a highly necessary form of remote control; for he had recently discovered, like his father before him, that you could see a lot of life if you kept right on walking.

Playing with David consisted largely of being towed at high speed round the garden, further and further afield.

After ten days, John said at breakfast: "Obviously, Sennacherib *didn't* find enough water in the Gomel river. Let's start."

So Hilda went off to organise food supplies, and John to arrange for a man and a mule to come with us; and David, straining at the leash, towed Rosaleen and me off on a rehearsal.

"I *do* hope I can manage it," she said. "I really loathe walking. It's all I can do to keep up with this child. Why can't we ride?"

I said that John would be horrified. The whole joy of travel in Greece for him was in beating the miles off underfoot. "And the end of each day makes up for *everything*," I added. Rosaleen thought it was not a very happy way of putting it.

"David doesn't think he'll come," John said, as we gathered at the garden gate the next morning. "I told him we were only going to amble—and he's in rather strict training just now."

"I wish he *could* come," said Hilda, looking fondly down on her son, already harnessed up for the serious business of the day—we should be away from him for about ten days. We waved to him and his nurse; for a moment he looked at us slightly morosely from beneath a round panama hat; then he gave a sudden flashing smile as a good idea for a new walk hit him, waved violently back, wheeled round and went beetling off across the garden, Nurse loping after him.

"I never saw such a busy back view," said John, and we went laughing off down the road past the Palace; the mule, loaded with tins and sleeping-bags and mackintoshes just ahead, led by a bronzed and saucy Cretan called Aleko. A little way past the Palace we left the road and crossed the valley over an ancient bridge; for the next ten days we found our way eastward along mule-tracks through the roadless heart of the island. It seemed even emptier and lonelier country than the mainland; we hardly saw anyone outside the small isolated villages; yet the valleys were worked to the full, the little stony fields tipping up as high as they could cling against the steep sides of the mountains. The lovely rhythm was under way again that I remembered from a year back—the cool, refreshing stretches along streams beneath olives and willows and birches; then the scorching pull up a stony track over a great hillside covered with low bushes, the scent of thyme and gorse strong in the hot sunshine; every now and then a glimpse of a misty sea stretched across a dip in the hills; then the drop again into a valley, with perhaps a distant view across it of the tiny village we were making for, on a far-away sky-line.

Rosaleen told me afterwards that the first day nearly killed her, and after the first mile or two she became filled with sadness at the thought of all the sharp stones she would have fallen over by the time we reached the eastern end of Crete. I was very tired myself by the evening as we came up the last slope towards a village perched high on the shoulder of a great hill, where John and Hilda thought we would camp for the night —and I was in fairly good training after the long walks at Khorsabad. I began to feel worried about her.

John asked the Headman of Skotino if we could sleep on his threshing-floor; and he escorted us just beyond the village, followed by the whole population. In Greece and Crete the threshing-floors are large circles of bare beaten earth surrounded by a low stone wall. This one looked extremely uninviting as a bedroom. But in a country where snakes coil through the bushes and soft grass, and much worse things turn up in most of the houses, the threshing-floor is the place to be. We lay down flat and rested, coats under heads, looking over the hills, all golden in the evening sun, to the far-away silken sea.

Shipmate.

The Grand Staircase in the Palace of Minos at Knossos.

Bronze head of Sir Arthur Evans at Knossos.

John with the Cretan guardian of Tylissos.

Cretan athlete somersaulting over bull.

Greek mainland at dawn—Full Circle.

"I can't believe I've stopped walking," said Rosaleen. "I don't think I shall ever be able to start up again."

We began to get the evening meal. The villagers brought bread and olives and cheese and great oranges, and we heated soup over a tiny stove and opened tins. Then the Headman came, proudly bearing a great flask of local wine. All round the low wall of the threshing-floor stood the villagers, three deep, the children being given the front row. They did not speak, just gazed. It was the most interesting thing that had happened to them in years, perhaps ever. We lingered over the meal and the wine, while darkness fell; and still they stood there. The stars began to pierce the high amethyst sky, and a waning moon climbed the eastern hills. And suddenly something happened to Rosaleen; the magic took hold and worked; all her fatigue and doubt was swept away on a draught of heady Cretan wine, as she realised the utter joy of reaching a lovely place after a hard day's going.

"This is the most perfect place, and the most perfect evening and the most perfect threshing-floor I ever knew in my life," she said, laughing happily, and everybody, villagers included, laughed too; and at last they left us and trailed away to their rest.

I can't say it was the most perfect night I ever spent—the ground was plaguey hard. In the middle of the night I remembered the days when I used to pore over 'Scouting for Boys'; and I sat up and found a knife in my bag, and dug a hollow in the ground, which is what all good Boy Scouts do to accommodate their hips when camping; and when it comes to hips I can give any Boy Scout points. It made all the difference—and all across eastern Crete I left a trail of little hollows in threshing-floors; and still hope that I didn't wreck the harvest that year for the puzzled villagers.

So we went on through that enchanted land; Rosaleen

flagging towards noon each day, but reviving at once after a glass of Cretan wine with her midday meal, to sail through the afternoon and evening on her toes, saying at intervals that walking was really wonderful, why had no one told her about it before?

After one of these midday pauses, John went off with a villager who said that he could show him some very ancient stones not far away in a field—for all the walks he did had an underlying purpose; he was gathering material for a comprehensive book about all the archaeological sites in the island. Hilda and Rosaleen and I used the time very comfortably by going fast asleep in a little grass plot under a shady tree just outside the village of Kalachorio, heedless of the giggles and whispers of several bullet-headed imps who had followed us. When we woke up, my hat had vanished. It was an ancient wide-brimmed faded sunhat, very much the worse for wear, for I had punched several holes in the crown by way of extra ventilation. It really didn't matter at all, I kept telling John, when he heard about it. But he took a very different view. He stopped dead, and marched us back to the village, and summoned the population. Hilda translated the impassioned speech that followed for our benefit: Was this Cretan hospitality? Could not a traveller shut an eye for one moment in this village of dishonour without fear of thieves? How could the villagers of Kalachorio ever hold up their heads again knowing that soon the villagers of London would be telling the tale: 'Have you heard? Those men of Kalachorio, in that island where once hospitality was a sacred trust, are found to be without honour.' For unless the lady's hat was returned within the day, the villagers of London would most surely hear of this shameful thing.

Kalachorio hung its head and shuffled its feet and said nothing. After a pause, John turned on his heel, all scorn and sorrow, and marched us off down the cobbled street. As we cleared the village, he grinned and said: "I *think* you'll get it back—bless them." He wasn't yet thirty, but already the Cretans, young and old, seemed to be his children.

That evening we reached Krasi—a tiny place high on a mountain; the small white houses rose in steps on either side of a steep narrow lane. We found a house for the night which had an open terrace alongside it. Then we walked on up to the top of the village to see the view; we were so high that the sea was clear of the hills and stretched golden from east to west, where long purple headlands reached far out into it against the sunset. There was a huge plane tree up there shading a lovely old arched hollow cut back into the mountain-side, and out of the rocky basin flowed the coldest and purest water I have ever tasted.

As we dropped down the steep street again in search of supper, we saw something very un-Cretan coming slowly up it—something very tall and thin in grey flannels and a pale yellow cardigan—Seton.

"How on earth did you find us?" John asked.

Seton said that he had reached the Villa the day before, and had discovered our general direction. He calculated how far we were likely to have got, and had hired a car to bring him along the coast road to about that point; and then had struck inland on foot, asking for news of us as he came.

"As soon as I got into the hills, everyone I met knew just where you were." The odd thing was that except for the last mile or so, his path hadn't crossed ours at any point.

We had supper on the terrace above the little street—and Seton drew pictures and diagrams to show us what the head of the canal looked like in the Gomel valley—for sure enough they had found it there, with a weir and sluice for controlling the river-water in and out of the canal, and huge sculptured blocks marking the entrance to it. And Jake had had himself lowered on a rope over the top of an appalling cliff because he wanted to copy inscriptions carved half-way down its face, while half a dozen Yezidis hung on to the rope at the top; and poor Rigmor had meanwhile gone on gallantly taking photographs of her lord and master dangling between heaven and earth, wondering all the time what the wild Yezidis' idea of a really good joke might not be. . . .

The owner of the house implored us to use his fine bedrooms that night. John and Hilda stuck firmly to the terrace in the open air. Rosaleen and I wavered, but the soft look of two dusty sofas in the front room on the first floor—up into which a flight of stairs rose straight from the street door—was too inviting to resist; and Seton, after a hard day's walking of nearly twenty miles, succumbed to the real bedroom behind. But not for long—Rosaleen and I were conscious of a long ghost, trailing rugs, stumbling across our room, murmuring: "An army of them coming at me up the wall," as he fled through the door on to the terrace.

Much later we woke again, as a clatter of hooves echoed between the street walls, and then a violent knock sounded on the door at the bottom of the stairs. I looked at my watch—it was nearly midnight. Rosaleen got up and peered through the tiny window, and the knock came again, louder. "It's a mule," she said. "It'll be up the stairs in a minute, I think."

I got up and we hung out of the window—and to our left three heads peered over the parapet of the terrace. The moon poured down on the white walls opposite, and on to the cobbles and the fantastic group below; for a dark Cretan in a great cloak sat there on a silvery mule, holding aloft a tall stick as if it were a lance—and perched on the point of it, like a gauntlet at a joust—my tattered old hat.

When he saw us all, he made a speech, explaining that at

sundown three small and wicked members of the village, not yet practised enough in honour and good manners, had broken down and confessed; whereupon the villagers had sent him at once to ride through the night and find us without fail. He could never go back to his people, waiting there so anxiously, unless he could take with him word that we would assure those villagers of London that the villagers of Kalachorio (with the possible exception of three small wicked ones) were men of honour.

John made a gracious speech back—somewhat blurred with sleep—and the stick was slanted towards me, and I removed its battered ornament. The rider wheeled about, saluting and smiling, and clattered off down the steep lane, a happy man; and we settled down again, with yet another joyful moment to remember.

The next evening found us down on the coast, camping on the empty shore below the Palace of Mallia, which lies tumbled among the flowers and grass, close to the sea. The fields along the shore were studded with little toy windmills on slender metal stalks, the ends of the white sails fixed to a circular frame of thin wire; I counted fifteen at least, and as a sea-breeze came bouncing inland at sunset, they all began merrily clattering and spinning, as fragile seeming as the paper ones on sticks at a fair. On the beach I picked up a small, beautifully worked hammer-head of polished green stone, which I have to this day—John said it was Neolithic, made probably somewhere about 3500 B.C.

Some men fishing near by brought us some of their catch for supper, including a very small octopus. As evening fell, the breeze died away completely, and we cooked supper over a fire of salty driftwood which spurted little brilliant fireworks of blue and green among the flames. And afterwards, propped in the soft sand round the faintly breathing embers, deeply content as we talked and smoked in the warm still air, Seton said:

"That hammerhead reminds me. I was looking for ibex one day in the mountains before we left, and as I was moving up a very narrow, high path—a ledge really—on one side of a narrow gorge, I suddenly saw an ibex moving on a path across the gorge. From where I stood I couldn't get a shot at it, and there was only one possible place, a few yards up where the ledge widened a little. I got there just in time to have a shot, but missed; and of course, that was that; he was off, never to be seen again. I marked the spot where he'd been when I fired, and climbed down into the gorge and up the other side to the spot, just as a matter of interest to see if I could find where the bullet had struck the rock-face, how near a miss it had been. I found the bullet hole quite easily—there was a white star all round it where chips of rock had splintered off. And look what I found an inch away from the bullet-hole."

He brought out of his pocket something small and long and pointed, and handed it round. It was a Stone Age arrow-head.

"It was half buried in the rock by the hole," he went on, "But enough was sticking out, at a slight angle, to show that the man who shot it must have aimed from exactly the same point as me—he'd probably gone through just the same frenzy of trying to reach the only possible spot in time; and in the flurry mucked it just as I did."

Hilda looked down at the slender flint, turning it over in the faint light of the fire, and then handed it back to Seton.

"Perhaps his ibex was an ancestor of your ibex," she said. "Just to round it off—I *do* hope so."

"A grand story," said John. "But I wish I knew how his Stone Age remarks compared with yours."

The next day we turned inland again, and climbed to a lovely village called Milatos, where every small house seemed to have a fountain of pink geraniums spilling over its white walls. They grew out of huge tins which had been painted as white as the walls, and fixed wherever there was a niche or a platform to take them. Some of the houses had old wooden stairs running up the outside, and here the geraniums foamed over on the upper landing of the staircase, overflowed down the side of the steps and cascaded through the balustrade, the great, scented heads and pale leaves swinging gently in the sunshine.

By the evening of that day a chilly breeze followed us in from the sea, and dark clouds rolled inland. We camped on a threshing floor close to a little white church, and John scanned the lowering sky.

"Only two more days' walking," he said. "Or one if we do the last bit by boat. I do hope we shall get to Seager's house before the weather breaks."

"Well, if it rains tonight we can move into the church," Seton said, "And I suppose, from what you tell me, that Mary will put her hip in the font."

The rain held off, and the next day was buoyant with sea-breezes and sparkling white clouds that rolled across a deep blue sky; and great shadows raced past us and up the steep and sunny hills. We walked a very long way that day; and in the evening breasted one last long hill and saw in the distance a cluster of little houses at the southern end of a great lake which lay in the shadow of high hills all around it.

"It's not really a lake," John said. "There are outlets north and south to the sea, into the Gulf of Mirabello."

In the middle of it lay a small white ship.

"That's the steam-yacht belonging to Imperial Airways," he said. "Sometimes the planes between Athens and Alexandria come down here."

We limped down the steep track; it took about an hour to

reach the waterside village. It was a poor little place, wedged between the hills and the water, and it didn't look as if there would be anywhere to camp even in the open; and Hilda was very dubious about trying any of the houses. It was when one stopped walking that fatigue really began to tell, unless one could rest at once. We stood uncertainly for a few moments on the quay, wondering what the next move had better be, limbs aching and insides very empty—and the air down here close to the water was chill. A small launch from the little white yacht was making its way to the quay, and we watched it idly as we discussed. The sailor at the tiller swung her neatly about and brought her gently to our feet. He made the craft fast, and hopped up on to the quay.

"Captain Poole's compliments," he said to all and sundry, "And he hopes you'll come aboard for dinner and stay the night!"

We goggled at him. How could they *possibly* . . .? But it must be sheer Cretan magic again, we thought, as we stepped dazedly down into the boat. The sailor opened up the throttle, and we spun round and away, chugging off towards the yacht. She was very spruce and bright, with "Imperia" in gold at her bow; and at the top of the gangway ladder stood a jovial little man in a white uniform with wild grey hair and a wild Irish eye.

"We've been expecting you for the last two days," said Captain Poole, welcoming us aboard. "Everybody on the water-side seemed to know that five crazy English people were heading this way through the mountains. Why walk, they say, when you can ride a mule?" I stole a look at Rosaleen. "So I kept a look out, and spotted you through field-glasses about an hour ago. Don't know how it's done, of course—wasn't as if they had drums or smoke-signals. It's a Godsend for us to have some company. Come and see your cabins—and then cock-tails." We found out that the three officers had turned out of their cabins and were going to sleep on deck; but they assured us that it was no hardship—they all seemed overjoyed at having fresh company to vary the monotony. It must have been a lonely job. They saw the passengers briefly when planes landed here, and that was all. Over cocktails, Captain Poole told us that he was also supposed to take *Imperia* smartly off to the rescue of any plane which might come down in difficulties between Athens and Alexandria.

"But we've never had a call in the two years I've been out here," he said. "And we couldn't go now, anyway."

"Why couldn't you?" we asked.

"Because we're hard aground on empty beer-bottles," he said. A gong sounded. "Dinner—come along."

We crowded into the tiny warm saloon. It was a wonderful dinner, and a wonderful evening. After coffee we sat on, elbows on table; and the good Cretan wine flowed, and the cigarette-smoke and talk eddied across the table; anecdotes from the merry Captain, tales of Egypt and Baghdad and Kurdistan from us. Rosaleen, half asleep, sat blissfully smiling, hardly able to believe that she had successfully tramped across half of eastern Crete, and that a real bunk, sheets and all, awaited her. Captain Poole said: "You people *have* travelled a lot," and she opened one eye, and said dreamily: "Oh! yes, we go for miles and *miles*."

We left early the next morning, as there was a plane due from Athens; and as we drew off, rested and gay, from the charming little white ship and our kind hosts waving at the rail, a great seaplane droned low over the northern mountain and settled on the smooth water, dwarfing *Imperia*, as she slowly taxied up alongside her.

Our walking was over—for we were all footsore, and voted to cut across the Gulf of Mirabello by motor-boat instead of walking round the long coastline. We said good-bye to Aleko and the good old mule, and transferred our baggage to a stout little tub of a boat, half decked-in, with the owner at the helm. Just as we were ready to start, a deputation approached to ask if we would give a lift to a local priest who wanted to get back to his village half-way down the Gulf. John and Hilda welcomed the dignified black-robed figure—his black, stove-pipe hat adding considerably to his already impressive height—as he crossed the quay and stepped down on deck. The deputation which had scurried back to a house to fetch him, now followed carrying a kitchen chair which was set down reverently in the exact middle of the deck, facing the stern. The priest bowed to us gravely, took his seat, and arranged his flowing garments; and we settled on the deck round his feet. The boat moved away from the quayside and turned south into a narrow channel between flat ground. At the southern end of the channel, where it passed into the open sea, a high spindly foot-bridge connected the two banks. It was raised well above the water to allow a good deal of clearance—but was it high enough, we suddenly all wondered, to clear that holy headgear now rapidly approaching it backwards? We were hypnotised into inaction—could only gaze fascinated at the calm bearded head soon to be dealt so rude and undignified a shock—the only thing we could hope to do was to field the stove-pipe as it sailed overboard.

The bow swept under the bridge—we held our breath—and then the stove-pipe glided after it, untouched, with two inches clearance, I should think. As we cleared the bridge the grave eyes, watching our faces change from agitation to relief, slowly crinkled up, and a great smile broke through the jungle beard—and he held up two fingers horizontally to show the margin of safety. We needn't have worried; he had obviously shot that bridge, sitting on that chair many and many a time, and had the whole matter in hand.

Now the water began to get very lively with a following wind, and the narrow chair wobbled a good deal—but that hazard, too, was surmounted, and soon we put the good man off on the western shore of the Gulf of Mirabello; he gave us his blessing from the quayside—and who knows that it did not bring us to safety through the next hour. For now the wind was whipping up big seas; we were making for a bay on the southern shore of the Gulf, called Pakhyammos, and as we neared it—a lee shore—huge green waves and clouds of spray were bursting up over dark, sheer rocks. The boatman was obviously being driven in nearer to the rocks than he liked; he kept leaning out over the side, his anxious eyes raking the blue-green turmoil round the small boat for signs of lurking rocks, and trying to force the bows seaward again. Very slowly we made headway past the rocks, and at last were clear; and then turned and drove straight for a smooth stretch of sand which opened up beyond them.

A path led up from the shore to a green plateau where trees grew, and among the trees we could see a long, green-tiled roof. At the top of the path a man and woman were waiting, the owner of the house and his wife. The American archaeologist, R. B. Seager, who had excavated the Minoan town of Gournia near by, had built the house, and had left it to this Cretan, Nicholas, on condition that he would keep it in readiness for any archaeological students who wanted to stay there, and look after them. Nicholas and his wife said that they had watched us coming across the water from afar, and had become afraid when sometimes the boat had disappeared in the troughs of the waves.

Soon we were safe in the beautiful house, resting in a flagged courtyard where the hot sunshine poured down, where geraniums of all shades of cream and pink and deep red grew in great green tubs, giant spires of blue and yellow lupins and clumps of lilies rose up against the white walls, and honeysuckle hung thick and fragrant over the pretty green doors.

Beyond the bay the huge dark mass of Mount Kavousi soared up, shutting off the easternmost tip of Crete; and we were content that it should be so. Our journey was well ended in this lovely place. For three days we rested in the sun, bathed in a tiny cove below the house, walked through the neatly laid out streets of ancient Gournia, in and out of its 4000-year-old houses, each with a trim doorstep at the street door; and in the evenings drifted up through the little village, past the lighted Taverna where there was always the sound of singing and a gentle guitar, up the path to the sheltered house; where at night the only sound was a nightingale bubbling among the curled amber fingers of the honeysuckle—and the endless whisper of the sea moving on the white shore.

. . . . . .

We went back to the Villa Ariadne by car; and one evening a few days later, after a farewell dinner in Candia, Rosaleen and I embarked on another little ship in the harbour. The night was blustery; there is always something desperately lonely about leaving the shelter of harbour on a rough night, moving away from the lighted houses and quayside, out into the great troubled dark—and now, too, we were sad for all that we had just left, the voices still fresh in our ears, the good company, the silly jokes, the utter beauty that we had moved through, the myriad scents of earth and flowers and sea, the whole magic of the ancient lovely island. We sought our cabin ruefully, and prepared for a bad night into the bargain; but somehow the rough sea lulled us quickly to sleep, and we awoke to a calm and brilliant day.

The southern horizon was empty—somewhere below that blue distance lay the purple mountains of Crete—lost for many years to come; but I knew even then that something of its spell would stay with me for ever. Perhaps I would come back again one day. Perhaps after all life didn't always move away in a straight, relentless line from happiness, like the wake of this little ship streaming away astern in a froth of cream and jade on the blue-black water.

I turned away, and looked forward. A little ahead on the starboard side a green island rose out of the sea, shimmering in the early morning sun. It was Milos; and a year-old memory stirred in me. Once again I was nearing the Greek mainland from the south, once again I was slipping past one of her quiet welcoming outposts.

I wasn't travelling away from happiness at all—I had simply come full circle.

Epilogue

'Already, I feel the bristles on my neck arising.' These words were my introduction to the vast desert of sand and stone which lies between eastern Iraq and Iran. They were spoken by Hans Frankfort (Dr Henri Frankfort), Director of the dig at Tell Asmar, as our car wobbled off the unmade road leading south from Baghdad.

It was my first encounter with the desert, one evening in October 1932, in my new job as secretary to the Director of the excavation, organised by the Oriental Institute of the University of Chicago.

Tell Asmar simply means 'Brown Mound' nowadays, and I have described at the beginning of this book the near-miraculous event of locating at Tell Asmar the previously completely lost whereabouts of ancient Eshnunna — already historically well-known to Assyriologists as an important vassal-city 5000 years ago to Ur, some 200 miles south.

Hans was a man of many interests ranging far beyond his academic achievements: yet these interests were linked, I think, in his teeming mind by a single great query: 'How did it all begin?' For instance, he dearly loved gardening and growing wonderful flowers: I remember him holding up a limp green shoot once which he was planting, and saying 'How does that know to be a snowdrop?'

He recoiled from the lifeless desert wastes where most of his archaeological fieldwork had to be done. (This will explain the opening words of this epilogue.) But in a sense they made a compelling unity with his total outlook on life. How did it all begin? How do plants become snowdrops? How do men begin to think and then try to explain things they could not then or now understand? How did different religions develop? And how and why did the people of Mesopotamia and Egypt, for instance, hold sometimes the same and sometimes quite diverse theories about the world they inhabited? And what inner urge drove early man to hack pieces of stone into the earliest sculpture ever found? Fearsome, somehow, in its primitive force and intention.

The work at Tell Asmar, as at other excavations, became gradually much more involved for me—and interesting—and well beyond my contractual obligations! (A curious and frequent phenomenon among the many who allow themselves to become absorbed beyond the humdrum side of their work.) The staff was large and multinational—American, Austrian, Danish, Dutch, English, Russian—among whom I made several lifelong friends.

Until the dig closed down, not long before the Second World War, we slowly unravelled the essence of ancient Eshnunna, from modern ground-level down to virgin soil about 30 feet below. It was a demonstration of ideal fieldwork, Hans interpreting each clue and 'find' with his historical wisdom, supported by his brilliant architects and etymologist, and a host of trained locals with their hoes and basket boys. We dug many other sites lying in our concession, but Eshnunna was the most important in confirming hitherto conjectural theories about the Dynasty of Ur.

Henri Frankfort died over 50 years ago, at the age of 57. His last book *Art and Architecture of the Ancient Orient* was published soon after his death. His books are still vital reading for students and archaeologists alike; and his conjectural opinions of how problems would arise and be solved after his time have never failed to be confirmed in later discoveries.

But will this desolate region, still with so much unknown treasure lying within its innumerable tell-tale mounds, ever be fully excavated? Has any, or much of it, re-irrigated in modern